P9-CQK-374

The Global Novel
Writing the World
in the 21st Century

COLUMBIA GLOBAL REPORTS
NEW YORK

The Global Novel
Writing the World in the 21st Century

Adam Kirsch

Canada
Margaret Atwood

Chile Roberto Bolaño

France
Michel Houellebecq

Italy Elena Ferrante

Turkey Orhan Pamuk

Japan
Haruki Murakami

Pakistan
Mohsin Hamid

Nigeria
Chimamanda
Ngozi Adichie

© 2017 Jeffrey L. Ward

Published by Columbia Global Reports
91 Claremont Avenue, Suite 515
New York, NY 10027
globalreports.columbia.edu
facebook.com/columbiaglobalreports
@columbiaGR

Library of Congress Control Number:
2016962876
ISBN: 978-0-9977-2290-1

Book design by Strick&Williams
Map design by Jeffrey L. Ward
Author photograph by Miranda Sita

Printed in the United States of America

The Global Novel
Writing the World
in the 21st Century

CONTENTS

World Literature and Its Discontents

There is a well-established rule for anyone writing about the increasingly popular, and surprisingly controversial, subject of world literature: Begin with Goethe. It was Johann Wolfgang von Goethe who invented the phrase "world literature," *Weltliteratur*, in a conversation recorded by his disciple Eckermann in 1827. His mention of the subject is brief, but it has founded a whole discipline: "I am more and more convinced that poetry is the universal possession of mankind, revealing itself everywhere and at all times in hundreds and hundreds of men.... National literature is now a rather unmeaning term; the epoch of world literature is at hand, and everyone must strive to hasten its approach."

Who could doubt that Goethe's prophecy has come true many times over? In the twenty-first century, almost two hundred years into the "epoch of world literature," the canonical

books of all languages and cultures have never been easier to
access. Whether you want to read the Gilgamesh epic, *The Tale
of Genji*, the Tibetan *Book of the Dead*, or *War and Peace*—or, for
that matter, Goethe's own works—they are all just a mouse-
click away. Nor have living writers ever had a more intimate and
up-to-date knowledge of the work of their contemporaries in all
parts of the world. A dedicated American reader of fiction today
is as likely to be familiar with the works of Haruki Murakami,
Elena Ferrante, or Roberto Bolaño as she is with the writers of
her own country. Technology, culture, and economics all seem
to predict that this union will grow ever closer. Barring a civili-
zational disaster, it's hard to see how literature could ever return
to a parochial or even merely national perspective.

But if "world literature" were really such a settled matter,
Goethe's words wouldn't continue to haunt the subject like a
guilty conscience. In fact, the more you think about his terms
and concepts, the more enigmatic they become. Does "the epoch
of world literature" mean simply an age, like our own, in which
many books, especially the classics, are available for reading?
Or did Goethe hope for something more—a truly cosmopolitan
literature, in which national origin would have ceased to matter
at all? Could such a thing ever exist, so long as people continue
to speak different languages? As long as they do, readers will
depend on translations—often translations into English, which
is the world's most popular second language. But is translation
a valid form of interpretation, or does it obscure more than it
reveals? Does the hegemony of English threaten the diversity
of literatures and cultures? And beyond the words on the page,
can the national and local context of a book be "translated" in

12   such a way as to make the text as meaningful to foreign readers as it is to its original audience? Goethe believed that national literatures were obsolete, but can a book ever be immediately global? Wouldn't a truly global literature depend on the abolition of difference altogether?

In this way, what might seem like strictly literary questions turn out to converge with the largest and most urgent issues of our age of globalization. The question of whether world literature can exist—in particular, whether the novel, the preeminent modern genre of exploration and explanation, can be "global"—is another way of asking whether a meaningfully global consciousness can exist. Perhaps the answer is already suggested by the question: It is only because we have grown to think of humanity on a planetary scale that we start to demand a literature equally comprehensive. The novel is already implicitly global as soon as it starts to speculate on or record the experience of human beings in the twenty-first century. Global novels are those that make this dimension explicit.

Of course, this does not mean that the global novel has superseded the novel of the city, or region, or nation. The global novel exists, not as a genre separated from and opposed to other kinds of fiction, but as a perspective that governs the interpretation of experience. In this way, it is faithful to the way the global is actually lived—not through the abolition of place, but as a theme by which place is mediated. Life lived *here* is experienced in its profound and often unsettling connections with life lived elsewhere, and everywhere. The local gains dignity, and significance, insofar as it can be seen as part of a worldwide phenomenon.

Indeed, the global novel is now the most important means by which literature attempts to reckon with humanity as such. The ambition to speak for and about human nature, which has been the object of critical suspicion for several generations, still flourishes among writers. The difference is that, where a novelist of the eighteenth century might simply assert the unity of human nature—as in Jane Austen's blithe "it is a truth universally acknowledged"—the twenty-first-century novelist must dramatize that unity, by plotting local experience against a background that is international and even cosmic. But both types of writer advance claims about the nature and destiny of our species. The fact that, in our time, these claims are frequently pessimistic—that they focus on themes of violence, alienation, and reckless exploitation—should not obscure the fact that writing the global novel means making a basic affirmation of the power of literature to represent the world.

It is because the stakes are so high that the academic and journalistic discussion of world literature is so impassioned, and usually so critical. Indeed, the banner of most writers on the subject could be inscribed with the title of a recent book by Emily Apter: *Against World Literature*. To be against world literature might seem like the ultimate impossibility for a literary scholar, whose vocation is based on reading across borders. Surely world literature is a perfect demonstration of the liberal values on which, all intellectuals depend for their existence— values like tolerance of difference, mutual understanding, and free exchange of ideas.

14

To be sure, Apter herself is not opposed to any of these things: "I endorse World Literature's deprovincialization of the canon and the way in which, at its best, it draws on translation to deliver surprising cognitive landscapes hailing from inaccessible linguistic folds." Put more simply, reading across borders opens our minds and gives us access to new ways of thinking and feeling. But Apter goes on to deplore "tendencies in World Literature toward reflexive endorsement of cultural equivalence and substitutability, or toward the celebration of nationally and ethnically branded 'differences' that have been niche-marketed as commercialized 'identities.'"

This is one of the commonest charges against world literature: By making foreignness into a literary commodity, it prevents the possibility of any true encounter with difference. In this way, it duplicates the original sin of translation itself, which brings the distant close only by erasing the very language that marks it as distant to begin with. Take "ethnically branded" writing: Once we think we know what, say, an Indian novel or a Latin American novel is bound to give us, we will seek out (or publishers will offer us) only books that match that pre-established image. Genuinely difficult or challenging books will go untranslated and unread. More dangerous still, they will go unwritten, as writers around the world begin to shape their work according to the demands of the global marketplace. In this way, literature approaches the total "substitutability" of a monoculture. Just as Starbucks tastes the same in Stockholm as it does in Los Angeles, so a Swedish novel like Stieg Larsson's immensely popular *The Girl with the Dragon Tattoo* reads exactly like a treatment for a Hollywood movie (which it then inevitably becomes).

This aesthetic critique of globalized literature goes hand in hand with a harder-edged political critique, such as the one advanced by in the literary magazine *n+1* in a much-discussed 2013 editorial, "World Lite." In this essay, the editors of *n+1* directly link the current flourishing of world literature to "global capitalism," an economic system which, it is implied, all people of good will must oppose. The writers who flourish in this system, who win prestigious prizes and occupy university chairs, are the beneficiaries of an unjust order: "World literature . . . has become an empty vessel for the occasional self-ratification of the global elite, who otherwise mostly ignore it." World literature is likened to the Davos Forum, a venue where celebrities and tycoons discuss "the terrific problems of a humanity whose predicament they appear to have escaped." Indeed, world literature has its own institutions—the Frankfurt Book Fair, multinational conglomerate publishers, international literary festivals, the Nobel Prize—which the editors consider to be inherently corrupt.

This hostile view of contemporary "world literature" and its leading lights—the editors of *n+1* name Salman Rushdie and J. M. Coetzee, along with younger writers such as Mohsin Hamid and Chimamanda Ngozi Adichie—sees its literary and political deficiencies as mutually reinforcing. The type of "world" writing celebrated today is abstract and deracinated: "A smooth EU-niversality prevails" in novels that are "extremely psychological in character and only vestigially social and geographical." The particularity of place and culture disappears, as well as formal difficulty of the kind associated with modernism. Along with them disappears the kind of political agenda

16 which the editors of *n+1* see as indispensable to a valid literary project: They regret the passing of "the programmatically *internationalist* literature of the revolutionary left." In both literary and political terms, the "smoothly global" is seen as the foe of "thorny internationalism," and the editors call for "*opposition* to prevailing tastes, ways of writing, and politics" all at once.

This line of argument can be seen as a form of nostalgia for the union of modernist aesthetics and radical politics that characterized the advanced intelligentsia in the 1930s and 1940s. That it took an effort of will to hold the two parts of that project together is something that "World Lite" tends to ignore. Difficult literature is almost never popular, which makes it an uncomfortable bedfellow for socialist politics; perhaps for this reason, the great modernists were more often sympathetic to fascism than socialism. The idea that literature can, and should, be both politically virtuous and aesthetically challenging is one of those ideals that, as the editors themselves say about socialism, "has so far enjoyed hardly a moment of historical realization." But for that very reason, this ideal can make actually existing world literature seem compromised and complaisant.

Interestingly, like many critiques of globalization, this attack on globalized literature can rally support from cultural conservatives as well as radicals. In a 2015 article, the American writer Michael Lind observes that "if the size of the global audience is the index," then the leading works of "contemporary world literature" are genre novels like Larsson's crime series or George R. R. Martin's fantasy series *Game of Thrones*. This is what Lind calls "world literature in the form of . . . popular culture," and it represents a kind of nightmare inversion of what

Goethe had in mind: not the best that has been thought and said, but the lowest common denominator.

To counter it, Lind calls for the restoration of a frankly elitist model of "global classicism." The global quality of such writing consists not in popularity across cultures, but a cosmopolitan appropriation of the best models of the past, regardless of their linguistic or national origin. Goethe himself, writing German lyrics based on the medieval Persian poetry of Hafiz, is a good example of this sort of cosmopolitanism. If such writing turns out not to appeal to a wide audience, so be it: Lind points out that Goethe envisioned poetry as the possession of "hundreds and hundreds of men," not hundreds of millions.

In an unexpected turn, however, Lind also employs this ideal of global classicism as a weapon against modernism, which he characterizes as an artistic movement that cut off writers and readers from literary tradition. Global classicism would, then, be formally conservative, as opposed to the radically innovative classicism of writers like Ezra Pound or James Joyce. It would produce "a genuine world literature far more erudite and refined than global popular culture." In this way, the attack on global literature can lead toward a cultural politics of restoration, a kind of intellectual protectionism in which writers guard their literary resources against competition from corporate behemoths.

The novelist and translator Tim Parks also argues that the winners in the game of world literature are mediocre books. But in a 2010 essay for the *New York Review of Books,* with the blunt headline "The Dull New Global Novel," Parks expands the critique from genre fiction to literary fiction itself. World literature is not just the name of a canon of great books, Parks argues; it is

18   also a market dynamic, in which authors come to define success as "an international rather than a national phenomenon." And "from the moment an author perceives his ultimate audience as international rather than national, the nature of his writing is bound to change. In particular one notes a tendency to remove obstacles to international comprehension." Local allusions and references disappear, along with the kind of complex word-play that is impossible to translate. Apter, resisting this kind of simplification, writes approvingly of "the Untranslatable," as a kind of wrench thrown into the smoothly turning gears of world literature: "Untranslatability [is] a deflationary gesture toward the expansionism and gargantuan scale of world-literary endeavors."

More fundamentally, Parks complains that "world litera-ture" gives writers an incentive to employ "highly visible tropes immediately recognizable as 'literary.'" (He instances the "over-stated fantasy devices" of Salman Rushdie and Orhan Pamuk, to which many examples could be added.) The global novel, if such a thing exists, is necessarily a diluted and deracinated genre, engaged not with reality but with the reiteration of its own themes and techniques. Against Goethe, this argument implies that "national literature" will always remain the most relevant context for any work of fiction. So long as life is lived locally—in a specific language and place, according to the mores and values of a unique society—global literature can only exist by abstract-ing away from these particularities. This is especially damaging in the case of the novel, which is traditionally the genre that engages most closely with social reality: "A new Jane Austen can forget the Nobel," Parks concludes.

A powerful and intriguing expression of this kind of pessimism can be found in *The Fall of Language in the Age of English*, by the Japanese novelist Minae Mizumura. First published in 2008, Mizumura's book-length essay set off a wide-ranging debate in Japan, as readers responded to her strongly worded disparagement of contemporary Japanese literature and the Japanese educational system. But while much of Mizumura's frame of reference is local—she writes at length about the origin of the modern Japanese novel—her wider argument can be applied to any national literature in the twenty-first century.

The idea of national literature itself, Mizumura speculates, may turn out to be only a brief parenthesis in the long history of literature. In most times and places, she argues, literacy required bilingualism: The language a writer spoke was not the language he used for writing books. This was equally true in medieval Europe, where Latin was the language of international philosophy and science, as in medieval Japan, where poetry and religious works were always composed in Chinese. The idea that a writer had a special, even spiritual relationship with his vernacular language was an invention of post-Renaissance Europe, from which it spread to other cultures around the world, including Japan.

But as we enter a future in which English is the dominant language of business, science, and scholarship—in which educated people around the world are expected to be bilingual in English, just as they once were in Latin or in Chinese—Mizumura fears that we may return to that older model. "Bilinguals," she predicts, will "start taking their own country's literature less seriously than literature written in English—especially the

20   classics of English literature, which are evolving into the universal canon." This will effectively mean the end of national
literature as a vehicle for major creative achievement. World literature will triumph, but at the price of linguistic diversity, and
all the mental diversity it makes possible.

Globalization, on this account, is another word for the
imperialism of the English language—whose dominion may
very well survive the hegemony of the United States, just as
Latin survived the fall of Rome. Its effect is to make writers of
all other languages feel provincial: "Japanese people at some
point, without even knowing it, became captive to the notion
that only Western languages are valid. Various non-Western
peoples share a similar sense of estrangement from their own
language," Mizumura writes. And the elevation of the English
language carries with it, almost accidentally, the elevation of
English literature. Indeed, she points out that even French literature, once the universal standard of literary style, is now a
more or less specialized interest: The world reads Shakespeare,
but not Racine. As a novelist who writes in a non-Western language, Mizumura is dismayed by this prognosis, but she is not
sure anything can be done to avert it.

In her analysis of the prestige and power dynamics of
national literatures, and the psychological toll these can exact
on writers, Mizumura owes a clear debt to the French literary
theorist Pascale Casanova. Indeed, Casanova's book *The World
Republic of Letters*, published in French in 1999 and in English
five years later, has become nearly as ubiquitous as Goethe in
discussions of world literature. It offers a new way of thinking

about literature as a form of symbolic capital, accrued by nations through the production of classic books, as well as through the development of a literary readership and the institutions which support it, like publishing houses and magazines. And just like any other resource, Casanova argues, literary authority is subject to intense competition between nations; she compares it to an "economy, which produces hierarchies and various forms of violence."

This violence is not physical, but spiritual, and it consists in the relegation of writers from smaller countries and language-groups to a literary periphery, subject to value judgments from taste-makers in the capital. For Casanova, this primarily means Paris, which for centuries was the center of the literary universe. Her most interesting insights have to do with the situation of writers from such "peripheral" places, and the challenge they face in escaping their perceived provincialism and winning the recognition of the "capital." Achieving a place in world literature, she argues, means escaping the provincial time-scale of most national literatures, which lag behind the avant-garde in terms of literary technique, and joining the "Greenwich meridian of literature," which has traditionally run through Paris. "The continually redefined present of literary life constitutes a universal artistic clock by which writers must regulate their work if they wish to attain legitimacy," Casanova writes—that is, legitimacy in the eyes of the metropolitan readers and critics who have the power to bestow it.

Casanova's new model of world literary space and time is meant to reveal the power struggles that are constantly

22 taking place under the apparently harmonious surface of literature. In this sense, it does for world literature as a system
what Harold Bloom's *The Anxiety of Influence* did for the psy-
chology of individual authors. Key to Casanova's insight is that
literary competition, though grounded in national and linguistic identity, is relatively independent of political rivalry. That
is, a country can accrue literary capital in excess of its geo-
political power—like France in the twentieth century—and,
conversely, a writer from the periphery (Joyce in Ireland, Kafka
in Czechoslovakia) can elude his or her political identity to
become an international figure. Indeed, it is only writers on the
literary periphery who perceive—because they are forced to—
the actual relations of domination and subjection that make up
literary space. Such "domination . . . is recognized as accepted
by outsiders while remaining wholly unknown to the inhabit-
ants of the centers"—just as an American reader, accustomed
to living in an English-speaking world, would never guess at the
anxieties that the English language causes a Japanese writer like
Mizumura.

But after Casanova has articulated the complex mecha-
nisms that governed international literary space in the modern
world—from the Renaissance until at least World War II—she
observes that the twenty-first century might turn out to be very
different. For one thing, Paris has lost its primacy as the gate-
keeper of world literature. Though many writers still come to
world attention through French translation, it is now possible
to appeal to centers in London or New York instead. More insid-
ious, however, is what Casanova—like several of the writers
we have seen—identifies as the rise of a new "world literature"

based on "denationalized content [which] can be absorbed
without any risk of misunderstanding."

Like the editors of *n+1*, Casanova opposes this new global
literature to the older model of "genuine literary internationalism." Whereas the world republic of letters used to be
constituted by innovation and rivalry, today it is dominated
by "international business," which produces an ersatz "'world
fiction,' products based on tested aesthetic formulas and
designed to appeal to the widest possible readership." It is easy
to hear in this complaint an echo of the Frankfurt School's
mid-twentieth-century attack on the American culture industry, which was said to mass-market kitsch in order to stupefy
the population into obedience. Like Theodor Adorno, contemporary critics of world literature bemoan the disappearance
of aesthetic originality and difficulty, and the corruption of
popular taste for the sake of corporate profit and control. In
Casanova's case, this takes the form of a (historically quite
familiar) defense of French and European values against
"American (or Americanized) large-scale literary production,
[which] . . . poses a grave threat to the independence of the
world of letters as a whole."

In theory, then, world literature sounds like a prescription for
disappointment and mediocrity. But does the reality live down
to the expectations and prophecies of the critics? The only way
to answer the question is empirically, by returning to the books
themselves. The following chapters examine eight novels that
have reached worldwide audiences in the twenty-first century,
by writers who are generally agreed to be leading figures in the

24   pantheon of world literature: Orhan Pamuk, Haruki Murakami, Roberto Bolaño, Chimamanda Ngozie Adichie, Mohsin Hamid, Margaret Atwood, Michel Houellebecq, and Elena Ferrante. While the list is inevitably partial, it is also intended to be representative; other studies of world literature today could include different books, but none could be complete without taking account of the work of these writers. They span six languages and five continents, and the variety in their narrative strategies and prose styles is just as great. Nothing unites them, perhaps, except contemporaneity and the shared status of being "global" novelists.

For this very reason, however, reading them together helps to reveal what it really means to talk about global fiction. And it offers a more hopeful picture of world literature than the one painted by critics and theorists. As it turns out, the global novels of our time are not passive products or victims of globalization; rather, they are acutely conscious of their position as part of a world system. Globalism is not just a fate thrust upon writers, but a theme that writers see it as a duty and an opportunity to explore. In very different ways, each of these writers addresses the question of what it means to write across borders. How can a writer situated in one culture communicate its truth to readers in very different places? Is it possible to generalize about human beings on the level of the species and the planet? Is literature impoverished by taking the whole world as its frame of reference, or enriched? How do contemporary global problems, including immigration, terrorism, environmental degradation, and sexual exploitation, appear through the lens of fiction?

What emerges from this kind of comparative reading is that the global novel is not a unitary genre. It is impossible to say that all global novels have certain formal qualities in common. On the contrary, the global is best thought of as a medium through which all kinds of stories can be told, and which affects their telling in a variety of ways. A global novel can be one that sees humanity on the level of the species, so that its problems and prospects can only be dealt with on the scale of the whole planet; or it can start from the scale of a single neighborhood, showing how even the most constrained of lives are affected by worldwide movements. It can describe a way of life common to people in many places, emphasizing the interchangeability of urban life in the twenty-first century; or it can be one that emphasizes the importance of differences, and the difficulty of communicating across borders. It can deal with traditional cultural markers like appearance and behavior or with elusive cosmic intuitions that seem to transcend place.

What unites all these various approaches is the insistence on the global dimension not just of contemporary experience, but of contemporary imagination. If we understand ourselves as citizens of the world, then the novel must come to grips with this cosmopolitanism—just as over the last three centuries it has explored each new iteration of "the way we live now." Ambitious novelists in the twenty-first century will find themselves writing global novels, not out of a cynical desire to elevate their commercial or critical rewards, but because individual lives are now lived and conceived under the sign of the whole globe. In the process, such writers will indeed encounter the problems of representation and homogenization that

26   criticism has been quick to point out. But such problems are not
      necessarily disabling; for the resourceful novelist, they can be
      stimulating and productive. To examine the global novel in its
      twenty-first-century variety is to be hopeful, if not for human-
      ity, then at least for the capacity of fiction to reveal humanity to
      itself.

The Ambassador: Orhan Pamuk's *Snow*

If any author has flourished in the twenty-first-century eco-system of world literature, it is Orhan Pamuk. Pamuk, born in Istanbul in 1952, writes in Turkish, a language whose literary achievements are generally unknown to the wider world. In this sense, Turkish is exactly a "national literature" in the sense Casanova and Mizumura intend—a literature that requires translation if it is to cross national boundaries. Indeed, Pamuk is a good example of what might be called the United Nations effect in world literature, whereby each country is allowed a single representative in the world's literary consciousness. Just as Albanian literature, for instance, means Ismail Kadare to most foreign readers, so most readers who encounter Pamuk in translation would likely be hard-pressed to name a second living Turkish novelist.

The writer who occupies this ambassadorial position, however, is often rewarded with fame on an impressive scale. Pamuk's novels have been translated into sixty languages and sold more than eleven million copies around the world. He received the Nobel Prize for Literature in 2006, the capstone of a series of major prizes awarded by judges in Germany, France, and England. Notably, the award of the Nobel followed a much-publicized criminal charge against Pamuk in Turkey, where he was accused of "insulting Turkishness," after giving an interview to a Swiss newspaper in which he referred to Turkey's crimes against the Armenians and the Kurds. This affair, which so notably contrasted European standards of free speech with Turkish ones, was an embarrassment to Turkey at a time when it was seeking admission to the European Union. The Swedish Academy's decision to honor Pamuk at just this moment was widely seen, especially in Turkey, as a rebuke of the charges against the novelist and a statement of support for free speech. In this way, Pamuk followed the pattern observed by Casanova, in which a writer from a small language group is able to appeal to an "international" (that is, Western European and American) literary community against the constricting standards of "local" literature.

As often happens with great writers, this episode in Pamuk's life was just like something that could have happened in his books. In particular, the conflict between Turkey and Europe, Islam and the West—and the meaning of this conflict for literature and politics—was the subject of what is often considered Pamuk's greatest book, *Snow*. This novel, published in Turkey in 2002 and in English translation two years later, was written, according to an author's note, between 1999 and 2001. It appeared in the aftermath of the September 11, 2001 attacks, which brought the themes of *Snow* front and center in the world's consciousness. In this way, a book that in one sense could not be more local—almost the entire novel takes place over a few days in a provincial Turkish city—turned out to embody the most urgent issues in global politics.

Indeed, the congruence of Pamuk's themes with Western concerns is one of the factors that has led critics of world literature to hold him in suspicion. When a Turkish writer undertakes to write about his country, knowing that his books will be read around the world and especially in Europe and America, does that automatically turn him into a kind of cultural translator or ambassador? If so, how does he avoid the double temptation of flattering his compatriots, to avoid denigrating his country in the eyes of the world, or of condescending to them, to cement his position as a world writer emancipated from the idols of the tribe?

No one is more conscious of these complications than Pamuk himself, who works them into the very structure of *Snow*. The novel tells the story of a poet, known by his initials as Ka, who spends a fateful few days in the city of Kars, a small city in eastern Anatolia near the border with Armenia. But it is narrated by a second writer, Ka's friend, a novelist whose name is revealed only halfway through the book to be Orhan. By compelling the reader to identify the narrator with the author himself, Pamuk creates the illusion that the story of Ka, which the narrator pieces together through interviews and research, is a true one. If so, that means the characters in the book must

32   also be real people; and this opens the possibility that Pamuk might allow them to speak for themselves. Indeed, on the next to last page, the narrator asks a character, Fazil, "what he might want to say to my readers if ever I was to write a book set in Kars." In this way, Pamuk creates the illusion of subtracting himself from his own novel: he cannot be guilty of misrepresenting Fazil, since Fazil is being given the opportunity to represent himself to the reader.

But what he says is not encouraging, either to Pamuk the novelist or to the non-Turkish reader. "If you write a book set in Kars and put me in it," replies Fazil, "I'd like you to tell your readers not to believe anything you say about me, anything you say about any of us. No one could understand us from so far away." This is practically the novel's last word, and it seems to represent an abdication on the novelist's part. After 450 pages of narrative, we are told that none of the people or places we have met are, or could be, truly represented in that narrative. And yet, of course, Ka, and Fazil, and "Orhan" himself, are all fictional characters, all creations of Pamuk; it is Pamuk who invents the character who refuses to be a character. In this way, he simultaneously acknowledges the impossibility of cultural translation—which is the foundation of "world literature"—and negates that impossibility, by allowing us to respond to Fazil as to a real person.

Pamuk's awareness of the barriers to full translatability is coded in the novel's very title. "Snow" is a fitting title for a book whose action takes place during a non-stop snowstorm. Ka's visit to Kars is regularly punctuated by descriptions of falling snow, and the snow becomes both a major plot point—it seals

off the city from the outside world, setting the stage for a local
military coup—and a thematic key. For Ka, who struggles with
Islamic belief just as he does with Turkish identity, snow is a
reminder of or surrogate for the existence of God: "What brings
me close to God is the silence of snow," he reflects. This silence
is an appropriately enigmatic sign of divinity, for a poet who can
neither fully believe nor disbelieve.

The Turkish word for "snow," however, is *kar*, which is the
novel's original title, and must be one of the most often repeated
words in the text. In Turkish, then, *kar* forms a linguistic bridge
between the protagonist, Ka, and the city, Kars: ka, kar, kars, a
pun that suggests a deep unity. But as Pamuk of course intended,
this pun is untranslatable. In English, you can hear the similar-
ity between Ka and Kars, but not the word for "snow" that unites
them. This gesture could be characterized as defiant, for the way
it builds untranslatability into a novel obsessed with cultural
translation. But it could equally well appear resigned to the fact
that, just as Fazil says, it is impossible to fully know a place, or a
book, from outside.

Ka's own story is designed to bring the fraught relationship
between Turkey and the West into focus. As the novel opens,
he is returning to Turkey for the first time in twelve years. He
has spent that time living in Frankfurt, Germany, as a political exile, thanks to his youthful involvement with left-wing
publications. By now, Pamuk makes clear, his political passions
have burned themselves out, and Ka lives for only two things:
poetry and love. Neither of these, however, is available to him
in Germany, where he lives a shabby, cloistered existence and
is unable to write. "The thing that saved me," he says, "was not

34   learning German. My body rejected the language, so I was able
     to preserve my purity of soul."

          Structurally, Germany functions in *Snow* much as
     Switzerland does in Dostoyevsky's novel of political intrigue,
     The Possessed. These Western countries are offstage havens,
     where plots are hatched; but for those plots to be set in motion,
     the characters and the story must leave the West and return
     to the homeland, Russia or Turkey. So it proves with Ka, who
     no sooner sets foot in Kars than he begins to write poems. The
     novel is punctuated by moments in which inspiration strikes
     Ka, who will break off in the middle of a conversation or a meal
     to write down the verses he hears in his head. Pamuk presents
     poetry in unapologetically old-fashioned guise, as a mystical
     visitation impervious to rational understanding. This effect is
     underscored by the way the novelist describes Ka's poems with-
     out ever quoting them: it is as though Ka's inspiration belongs
     to a higher plane which the novel cannot access.

          So far, Pamuk seems to be presenting a kind of nineteenth-
     century nationalist theory of literary inspiration. Ka the poet,
     like Antaeus, loses his strength when cut off from his native
     soil. Only in Turkey—and not metropolitan Istanbul, but the
     "deep" Turkey of provincial Kars—does his imagination begin
     to function again. The same goes for his affections: Loveless in
     Germany, Ka makes for Kars in part because he hopes to find
     Ipek, a beautiful woman he once knew; and on finding her, he
     falls immediately and spectacularly in love. Here, again, Pamuk
     risks a naive, primal characterization of love, just as he did with
     poetry: Ka doesn't need to know Ipek to love her, indeed he
     loves her all the more because she remains mysterious, a symbol

of the eternal feminine. (No fewer than four male characters in
the novel love her, including Orhan, who finds himself reenact-
ing his friend's passion.)

Finally, if Kars brings Ka's imagination and passion back to
life, so it reawakens his instinct for belief. To fully understand
the ideological and religious forces at play in *Snow*, it's necessary
to know something about the modern history of Turkey—in particular, the way Kemal Ataturk, the founder of the modern state
in the 1920s, engaged in a forced secularization of a traditionally
Islamic country. This resulted in the creation of a secular elite,
which dominated the state and the army, and also the Istanbul
bourgeoisie, of which Ka is a product. But by the 1990s, when
Snow takes place, Turkey is witnessing a resurgence of political
Islam, in which provincial people like those in Kars are reas-
serting their religious identity. All of this creates complex
cross-currents in politics and religion, which would be extremely
familiar to Pamuk's Turkish readers, but requires interpretation
for his readers abroad. Pamuk walks a fine line here: he does not
spell out the basics of Turkish history and culture, but he allows
the unfamiliar reader to grasp their basic dynamics.

The immediate reason that Ka has come to Kars, he tells
everyone, is to write about the disturbing phenomenon of the
"suicide girls." In a plot strand based on real-life events, several young women in Kars have committed suicide, for no clear
reason, or rather for many—poverty, abuse, forced marriage,
despair. But in popular opinion, the girls are taken to be martyrs
for the cause of Islam: One of them, Teslime, had been involved
in a school protest, when she refused to take off her headscarf
as required by the secular school director. Early in the novel,

36   Ka happens to be in a café when the director is assassinated by
      an Islamic radical, intent on taking revenge for the death of the
      "headscarf girl."

          Ka's loyalties in this complex situation are torn. On the one
      hand, he is himself a nonbeliever, with a Western education and
      Western literary values, who has spent years living in the West.
      He is a natural supporter of Turkish secularism against politi-
      cal Islam. At the same time, the girls' headscarf protest can also
      be seen as a democratic, even feminist, assertion of individual
      conviction against the overbearing Turkish state. Then there is
      the problem of how identity—the public profession of secular-
      ism or religion—corresponds, or fails to correspond, with the
      lived experience of faith and doubt. Pamuk repeatedly suggests
      that belief itself means something different in Turkey than it
      does in the West. European religion is a matter of individual
      conviction, but in Turkey being a Muslim is above all adher-
      ence to the people and its way of life. "In this part of the world,"
      Ka reflects, "faith in God was not achieved by thinking sublime
      thoughts . . . nor was it something one could do alone; above all
      it meant joining a mosque, becoming part of a community." In
      a discussion with a charismatic religious leader, Ka longs for a
      way to reconcile his "Western" desire for independence with his
      "Turkish" longing for belief: "I want a God who doesn't ask me
      to take off my shoes in his presence and who doesn't make me
      fall on my knees to kiss people's hands. I want a God who under-
      stands my need for solitude."

          The action in *Snow* largely consists of Ka being lectured,
      bullied, and manipulated by competing factions in Turkish
      politics and religion. On the one hand, there is the actor Sunay

Zaim, who turns the performance of a secularist play (bluntly titled *My Country or My Headscarf*) into a real-life coup, when he orders soldiers onstage to turn their weapons on the Islamist students in the audience. What follows is several days of suspended reality, as the city is cut off from the outside world and Sunay is able to wreak havoc on Kars. His opposite number, equally violent in principle though much more likable as a person, is the Islamic terrorist Blue, who is living in hiding in the city. Ka has interviews with both of them, and with various other policemen, politicians, and students, all of which open up to the reader the schisms within Turkish society.

But hanging over every division and controversy is a maddening complication: the acute awareness of how these issues will appear to a "Western," non-Turkish audience. The literary issue of translatability is, in *Snow*, also a political and religious issue. No one in the novel can act unself-consciously; everyone is aware of how his actions and words might appear to the rest of the world. To Blue, the real motive for fundamentalist terrorism is not so much piety as the need for autonomy and self-esteem. "Most of the time it's not the Europeans who belittle us," he tells Ka. "What happens when we look at them is that we belittle ourselves."

Interestingly, Blue makes this point in explicitly literary terms, when he recounts for Ka the medieval legend of Sohrab and Rustum: "Once upon a time, millions of people knew it by heart—from Tabriz to Istanbul, from Bosnia to Trabzon—and when they recalled it they found the meaning in their lives. The story spoke to them in just the same way that Oedipus' murder of his father and Macbeth's obsession with power and

38   death speak to people throughout the Western world. But now, because we've fallen under the spell of the West, we've forgotten our own stories."

World literature, from Blue's perspective, means the global hegemony of Western stories. And in fact, this hegemony seems to be enacted in the pages of *Snow* itself, though in a covert way. One of the running jokes in *Snow* involves Ka's invention of a fictional German reporter named Hans Hansen, who is allegedly ready to print statements from the various factions in Kars in a Frankfurt newspaper. What Pamuk never says, but evidently hopes the reader will recognize, is that Hans Hansen is the name of a character in Thomas Mann's great story "Tonio Kroger," where he represents the healthy, incurious, normal life that remains inaccessible to the artist. Ka and Pamuk seem to be drawing their allusions from classic Western literature, not Eastern literature as Blue would prefer. Could it be that the novel itself is a Western genre—that to write novels like *Snow* is already to enlist in one party in the culture war Pamuk depicts?

Blue's embrace of Islam is supposed to signal his rejection of Western standards, according to which Turkey will always be inferior. Yet as Pamuk fully understands, this rejection of the West is just another stage in the dialectic of Western domination. If Blue is a terrorist in order to reject the West, his actions are just as much under the thrall of the West as those of a secularist bourgeois like Ka. Likewise, Ka can never know to what degree his own secularism, and his own modernist poetic standards, are a result of indoctrination by the standards of the West. Here Pamuk makes a legible symbol of Ka's overcoat, an expensive garment purchased in a German department store.

Everywhere he goes in Kars, people comment on it: its very quality marks it as a foreign article, and thus a declaration of allegiance to Europe. But would Ka be better off going without it and freezing? Can't a coat just be a coat?

In *Snow*, the answer seems to be that it can't. To be a Turkish writer like Ka, or like Pamuk, is to exist in a state of overdetermination. Every literary, religious, and political choice must be made self-consciously, in the knowledge that it reflects a certain stance toward Turkey and the West. Yet there remains the hope that the novel itself might be a genre that encompasses these divisions, not by transcending them in the name of a universal art, but by allowing all points of view to express themselves. "When a good poet is confronted with difficult facts that he knows to be true but also inimical to poetry," Pamuk writes, "he has no choice but to flee to the margins." The margins, perhaps, are where the novelist too belongs. He can belong wholeheartedly to no camp or party, but he can be the medium through which all people find expression.

Alternate Realities: Haruki Murakami's *1Q84* and Roberto Bolaño's *2666*

In *The Fall of Language in the Age of English*, Minae Mizumura offers a harsh judgment on the state of Japanese literature. "Representative works of today's Japanese literature," she writes, "often read like rehashes of American literature—ignoring not only the Japanese literary heritage but, more critically, the glaring fact that Japanese society and American society differ. One hundred years from now, readers of those works will have no idea what it was like to live in the current Heisei period (starting in 1989) of Japan." Like many other critics, Mizumura sees Americanization as a synonym for deracination, commodification, and dumbing-down: "Works of contemporary fiction tend to resemble global cultural goods, which, like Hollywood blockbuster films, do not require language—or translation—in the truest sense of the word."

The name of Haruki Murakami does not appear in this passage, or in Mizumura's book at all. But when she writes that "Japan's best and brightest have turned their backs on literature," there is a pointed and inevitable reflection on Murakami, who is by far the most popular novelist writing in Japan today. In 2009, when he published *1Q84*, a huge novel in three parts, it immediately became one of the best-selling books in Japanese history, selling a million copies in just one month. Murakami's celebrity in his native country is almost matched by his popularity abroad. His work has been translated into fifty languages, and he is often named as a leading candidate for the Nobel Prize.

Yet in 2014, Murakami told an interviewer that he considers himself "a kind of outcast of the Japanese literary world," an "ugly duckling" who has never been embraced by writers and critics. Indeed, the criticism leveled at Murakami by the Japanese literary establishment has been remarkably consistent. As the *New York Times* summarized it, "in Japan, the traditional literary critics regard his novels as un-Japanese and look askance at their Western influences, ranging from the writing style to the American cultural references." Murakami's interest in American culture and literature is indisputable. He has translated a wide range of American writers into Japanese, from Raymond Carver to F. Scott Fitzgerald, and he spent several years living in the United States.

But in a world literary ecosystem where the domination of the English language is seen as the source of many ills, Murakami's very success in and with English inevitably becomes a point of criticism. In a *Paris Review* interview, Kenzaburo Oe, the Japanese novelist who won the Nobel Prize in 1994, made the

44   point diplomatically, saying, "Murakami writes in a clear, simple Japanese style. He is translated into foreign languages and
is widely read, especially in America, England, and China. He's
created a place for himself in the international literary scene
in a way that Yukio Mishima and myself were not able to." The
compliment barely conceals the implication that Murakami's
success abroad is owed precisely to his simple, or simplified,
language. Rather than mastering the full resources and history
of the Japanese language, the way Oe and Mishima did, the sug-
gestion is that Murakami writes a version stripped for export.
Japan Today made the same argument in so many words, writing
that Murakami's success was owed to "the continued hegemony
of American publishing interests who understand that English
readers have little tolerance for the foreign."

In a sense, then, Murakami serves as a test case for the
aesthetic and even moral validity of global literature as a project. When a novelist writes books that are equally popular in
Tokyo, Los Angeles, and Athens, does he prove that twenty-
first-century life in all these places is fundamentally similar,
and therefore mutually comprehensible—perhaps even inter-
changeable? Or is this universality really just a lowest common
denominator—the manipulation of a set of conventions and
references that everyone understands because they have been
drilled into us by the global culture industry? Can there be a
global novel that is at once richly textured and widely legible, or
is there always a trade-off between these values?

1Q84, Murakami's biggest book, is an ideal text for con-
fronting these questions, since its perspective is at once
local—almost the entire story takes place in Tokyo—and

cosmic—playing with questions about the fundamental nature
of reality, and whether that reality is permanent or mutable.
It is also, not coincidentally, a book about the writing and
publishing of fiction. At the core of *1Q84* lies a novel-within-
the-novel called *Air Chrysalis*, a short manuscript that is
submitted to a literary contest. Its author, Fuka-Eri—the pen
name of Eriko Fukada—is a seventeen-year-old girl with no
previous experience in writing. Indeed, we soon learn that
she is actually unable to write; she is severely dyslexic, and
the manuscript was actually dictated to a friend, who surrep-
titiously entered it for the prize. Murakami emphasizes that,
technically and stylistically, Fuka-Eri's "writing" is amateur-
ish, incompetent. "First of all, look at this style," says Komatsu,
the editor who plucks the manuscript from the slush pile. "No
amount of work is going to make it any better. It's never going
to happen. And the reason it's never going to happen is that
the writer herself doesn't give a damn about style; she shows
absolutely no *intention* of wanting to write well, of wanting to
improve her writing."

Yet as badly written as *Air Chrysalis* might be, Komatsu
is certain that its story is compelling and potentially popular.
That is why he enlists Tengo, one of the novel's two main characters, to rewrite the manuscript, giving it a professional polish
that will make it worthy of publication. Tengo, a novice writer
who earns his living teaching mathematics in a cram school, is
at first reluctant to take on the job, seeing it as a species of fraud.
But he is soon deeply engaged in the task, which he finds cre-
atively liberating; and thanks to his efforts, *Air Chrysalis* does
indeed become a bestseller.

46   In telling this story, Murakami displays what might be
taken for cynicism about writing and publishing. Komatsu is
an author's satirical portrait of the editor as manipulator. Yet
Murakami plainly does not mean for the reader to be offended
by Tengo's rewriting of Fuka-Eri's novel. The fraudulence,
if any, is merely technical. In a deeper sense, the two are col-
laborators, and their collaboration is legitimate because of
a distinction that Murakami embraces, though most critics wouldn't—the distinction between form and content. It
is possible, Murakami suggests, for a book to be deficient in
style—the very charge lodged against his own books by some
Japanese critics—and yet to have a universal appeal, thanks to
the originality and inventiveness of its story. In a sense, writing
fiction is a joint effort between the imagination, which is primal
and untutored, and the intelligence, which is dedicated to craft
and technique. In *1Q84* these roles are played by two different
people, but Murakami implies that the same two faculties exist
within individuals as well.

          This is also, unmistakably, the wager of *1Q84* itself.
Stylistically, the book is plain, almost impoverished. Its length
is partly the product of repetition and redundancy: for instance,
there are very many scenes in which a solitary individual pre-
pares a meal, whose ingredients Murakami always lists with
painstaking completeness. Outfits are described as if they came
out of a catalogue—color, cut, name brand. But the book's size
is also owed to Murakami's spacious sense of scale and pacing,
which are reminiscent of the nineteenth-century serial novel.
Over the course of more than 1,100 pages, plot points are frequently recapitulated. There are long scenes in which characters

explain to one another exactly what is going on, a useful technique in a book replete with supernatural mysteries.

As for characterization, Murakami's people often have the sleek one-dimensionality of movie characters. This is especially true of Aomame, who joins Tengo as the novel's main focus—the two of them are subjects of alternating chapters for most of the book. Aomame seems to have stepped out of the pages of a comic book, or the frames of a spy movie. She is a sexy assassin, much given to lesbian fantasies and contemplating her own breasts, whose mission in life is to kill men who are guilty of abusing their wives. As the novel opens, we see her en route to her latest assignment, where she commits righteous murder using her trademark weapon—a long needle that she inserts into the brain of her victim, killing him instantly and painlessly. She is sent out on missions by an elderly woman known as "the dowager," a mastermind who uses her vast wealth to track down abusers. This phase of the novel has the exciting implausibility of genre fiction, and Aomame is at least a cousin to Lisbeth Salander, the avenging angel of Stieg Larsson's popular books.

At the core of *1Q84*, however, there is a kernel of strangeness that elevates the surrounding machinery, which is often workmanlike at best. This has to do, again, with *Air Chrysalis*, which plays a major role in the plot for hundreds of pages before we actually get a summary of its contents. The book Fuka-Eri has written turns out to be a straightforward, ostensibly factual account of an alternative reality, in which human beings share the earth with a race of supernatural creatures known as the Little People. These Little People have the power to weave a kind of cocoon out of the air—thus the title *Air Chrysalis*—which

48   they use to create copies of human beings for their own inscrutable, probably nefarious purposes. Murakami deliberately
leaves much about the Little People—their origin, their powers,
their purposes—vague and uncertain. This not only increases
their ominous power, but keeps *1Q84* from entering the ter-
ritory of science fiction, with its industriously worked-out
imaginative laws. Murakami is more interested in atmosphere
and evocation than in creating a mythology.

The insignia of the alternate reality, as described by Fuka-
Eri, is that its night sky contains two moons. At first this seems
like a mere fictional invention; but soon enough, first Aomame
and then Tengo discover that they can see two moons themselves. At some point, the novel's present, set in the year
1984, has branched off into the other world Aomame dubs, in
an untranslatable Japanese pun, 1Q84. Broadly speaking, the
suspense of the novel comes from the question of whether
Aomame and Tengo will be able to find one another and escape
1Q84. Along the way, they must battle supernatural forces and
a Little People-worshiping cult. They are aided in their quest
by the unconquerable power of love, which Murakami invokes
in an epigraph from the Tin Pan Alley song "Paper Moon": "It's
a Barnum and Bailey world/just as phony as it can be./But it
wouldn't be make-believe/if you believed in me."

This epigraph is the first cue that the cultural frame of reference Murakami employs in *1Q84* will be largely American
and Western. In the novel's first scene, Aomame is wrenched
out of the real world into 1Q84 as she sits in a taxicab listen-
ing to Janacek's *Sinfonietta*; this piece of Czech classical music
becomes a kind of theme song, recurring in various connections

throughout the book. (The popularity of *1Q84* actually created a vogue for the piece in Japan.) Later, characters read and discuss Chekhov and Proust and of course George Orwell, whose *1984* is one of Murakami's prime inspirations; they listen to Nat King Cole and Vivaldi. Culturally, Murakami suggests—and not polemically, but simply by matter-of-fact description—Japan is part of the West, speaking the *lingua franca* of Western culture. Significantly, the only character who lays claim to any kind of traditional Japanese culture is Fuka-Eri, who is able to recite long passages from the medieval epic poem *The Tale of the Heike*. This is presented as a freakish, almost idiot savant–like ability, and a sign of Fuka-Eri's profound divorce from the actual, modern world.

When it comes to modern life, Murakami offers a diagnosis that emphasizes its isolation and emotional poverty. Both Tengo and Aomame are profoundly solitary people, without family ties or real friendships. They work at jobs because they have to, and they largely enjoy their work—he is a math teacher, she is a physical therapist—but this work has little to do with their inner lives or real personalities. They live alone in small apartments, cook for themselves, and only rarely venture out to bars or restaurants. Indeed, Aomame and Fuka-Eri, as well as a fourth important character, the private detective Ushikawa, spend long stretches of the novel in hiding—a condition that seems almost like a natural extension of their ordinary lives.

1Q84, then, is a long but deliberately underpopulated novel. It operates on two levels, that of the isolated individual and that of the cosmos; Tengo and Aomame are on their own beneath the two moons. Almost totally missing from the book—indeed, almost

50   unimaginable on its terms—is anything like politics, history, or
     society. The Tokyo of *1Q84* is a city out of history, or after it, as
     Aomame reflects late in the novel: "She only watched TV twice
     a day—the NHK news broadcasts at noon and at seven p.m. As
     always, nothing big was going on—no, actually, lots of big events
     were happening in the world. People all around the world had lost
     their lives, many of them in tragic ways—train wrecks, ferry boats
     sinking, plane crashes. A civil war went on with no end in sight,
     an assassination, a terrible ethnic massacre. . . . Aomame deeply
     sympathized with the people caught up in these tragedies and
     disasters, but even so, not a single thing had occurred that had a
     direct bearing on her."

     The detachment of Murakami's characters is not neces-
     sarily intended as social commentary. There are biographical
     reasons why Aomame and Tengo are as lonely as they are, and
     it serves Murakami's purpose to emphasize their loneliness
     in order to make their final reunion sweeter and more intense.
     But it is unmistakable that this stripping down of the texture
     of social life—like the accessibility of his prose style—is one of
     the things that makes *1Q84* so translatable, and so amenable to
     being read as a global novel. Murakami does not deny place—the
     book is full of details about Tokyo neighborhoods, highways,
     train stations—but he does implicitly deny the significance
     of place. The characters of Pamuk's *Snow* couldn't exist any-
     where but Turkey, so deeply are they in the grip of its history
     and mystique; but the urban isolates of *1Q84* could almost as
     easily be living in New York or London. Culture, technology, and
     psychology combine, for Murakami, to create a modern life-
     style that is contentedly rootless. The worldwide success of his

books suggests that this insight captures something real about the way we live and read now.

In 2004, five years before *1Q84* was published in Japan, the similarly named *2666* appeared in Spanish. *2666*, too, was a novel in parts—its author, Roberto Bolaño, originally envisioned the book's five sections being released as separate volumes. But Bolaño died in 2003, at the age of fifty, and his heirs decided to publish the work as a single long book. Like *1Q84*, *2666* seems to bear the name of a year—in this case, a year in the distant future, rather than the recent past. But it is characteristic of the difference between the books that, while Murakami explains just what 1Q84 designates, the date 2666 does not appear at all in Bolaño's novel. Like so much in the book, it remains a mystery, speaking of a buried logic or a hidden perspective that might unite its wildly proliferating stories.

If 2666 is a year, it sounds like an ominous one, containing as it does the traditional number of the Beast from the Book of Revelations. And the dominant mood of Bolaño's magnum opus is certainly apocalyptic. Like Murakami, Bolaño operates on the level of the cosmic, suggesting—through metaphor and imagery, as much as through plot and character—that the world he writes about is fundamentally disturbed, a place of evil past, present, and to come. From the Holocaust in the 1940s to the epidemic of murders of women in 1990s Mexico, Bolaño is drawn to times and places where that evil comes undeniably to the surface, turning the real world itself into a surreally menacing alternative reality. It is in this spirit that, late in the book, a character looks at the night sky and sees it as an insignia of

52   the terrifying inescapability of history: "When these stars cast their light, we didn't exist, life on Earth didn't exist, even Earth didn't exist. This light was cast a long time ago. It's the past, we're surrounded by the past, everything that no longer exists or exists only in memory or guesswork is there now, above us, shining on the mountains and the snow and we can't do anything to stop it."

By insisting that we ourselves inhabit the worst reality—rather than quarantining evil into a parallel dimension, as Murakami does with his haunted 1Q84—Bolaño produces a book that is never simply entertaining, and often actively burdensome to read. This thorny ambition is consistent with his open contempt for the notion that a writer's calling is anything but the creation of masterpieces: "By now I knew that it was pointless to write, or that it was worth it only if one was prepared to write a masterpiece. Most writers are deluded or playing." Such a point of view on writing directly contradicts Murakami's sense, as captured in the character of Fuka-Eri, that a writer combines an imaginative seer with a practical craftsman. Every moment of a novel, Bolaño suggests by precept as well as his own practice, must work the fantastic into the very texture of the prose, if it is to do justice to the ominous strangeness of our world.

The terms of engagement with the world mark another significant difference between these two writers, each of whom has attracted an international readership. Murakami insisted on Aomame's sense that the news she sees on television has nothing to do with her own life. Indeed, the fantastical nature of her adventures can be seen as the replacement for the absence of history from her life. This sense of detachment from history is a faithful reflection of the experience of most people in powerful and prosperous First World countries, particularly Japan, with its postwar history of international neutrality. Bolaño, on the other hand, lived on both sides of the divide between history and post-history. The first half of his life, from 1953 to 1977, he spent in Latin America: first Chile, where he was born, then Mexico, where he began his literary career. In this time and place, Bolaño the writer was inevitably thrust into political commitments—indeed, he claimed to have been imprisoned in Chile in 1973, following the right-wing coup by Augusto Pinochet. In 1977, however, he moved to Europe, and spent most of the rest of his life in Spain, effectively in exile from the literary and political conditions of Latin America.

2666 sharply reflects Bolaño's sense that the world is divided into zones of immunity and vulnerability. If, to interpret his title, we are all on the path to the cataclysm of the year 2666, then different parts of the world are progressing toward disaster at different rates. In the 1990s and early 2000s, when most of the novel is set, Europe is a zone of peace, culture, and self-absorption. Its representatives are the four professors who dominate the novel's first part, "The Part About the Critics." Each of these characters comes from a different Western European country—they are English, Spanish, French, and Italian—and each is an expert in the work of a reclusive (and invented) German writer, Benno von Archimboldi. They live in an E.U. where national borders have ceased to be menacing— they are constantly flying from city to city to visit one another or attend scholarly conferences—and those borders now provide

54   only the slight piquancy of manageable difference. Similarly, the love quadrangle that emerges, as the three men in various ways pursue the only woman, belongs to the pacific genre of comedy.

Being European, Bolaño suggests, means occupying oneself with study and with love—a kind of end of history of the spirit. If these writers are critics and not creators—if they are doomed to a parasitic relationship with literature—this may be a small price to pay for emancipation from the terrible history that sponsors creation. Still, the novel does not forget that this postwar European paradise is of recent date, and that it may only conceal the permanent human drives toward violence. This becomes clear in one of the first part's most significant episodes, when two of the critics—the Spanish Espinoza and the French Pelletier—are in a taxi in London with the Englishwoman they both love, Liz Norton. As they discuss their love triangle, in which the two men tacitly agree to share the woman between them, their Pakistani taxi driver overhears and erupts in disgust: "in his country they had a word for what she was, the same word they had for it in London as it happened, and the word was *bitch* or *slut* or *pig*." As soon as their hypercivilization is challenged, Espinoza and Pelletier erupt in violence, beating the taxi driver nearly to death. It is a telling scene, in which Bolaño reveals the way European tolerance, in matters of sex and gender, turns into, or is identical with, aggressive intolerance of those foreigners and immigrants who do not share it.

In time, however, the critics are drawn out of Europe and into the place Bolaño proposes as the sick heart of contemporary reality: the fictional city of Santa Teresa, closely based on Ciudad Juarez, on the Mexican-American border. Santa Teresa, which will come to dominate the remainder of the book, is a creation of the globalized economy, with all its moral contradictions. Superficially, it is a thriving place, where poor people from all over Mexico come to find work in the *maquiladoras*, the foreign-owned factories which produce goods for export. Yet this economy creates a poor and transient population which proves to be highly vulnerable—to government corruption, drug gangs, and above all to the terrifyingly random and seemingly unmotivated murder of women.

Bolaño allows us to see Santa Teresa from several foreign points of view, before plunging the reader directly into the heart of its violence. The critics, who arrive there in pursuit of their reclusive idol Archimboldi, seldom leave their hotel and remain in the detached role of tourists. In the next section, "The Part about Amalfitano," Bolaño focuses on another immigrant, a Spanish university professor who has come to teach in Santa Teresa, and who is being slowly driven mad by the place. The third section, "The Part about Fate," introduces us to an American reporter, Oscar Fate, who comes to Santa Teresa to cover a boxing match but is drawn against his will into a fascination with the killings—and with Amalfitano's daughter, Rosa, who is just the kind of young woman who is most vulnerable.

Finally, in part four, "The Part about the Crimes," Bolaño brings the murders to the center of the narrative. He does this in blunt and unremitting fashion: For hundreds of pages, the narrative consists of short summaries of murder cases, as in a police blotter. Bolaño reports how a body was found, its condition of decomposition and injury, how it was identified (or remained anonymous), and how the police, after a brief and half-hearted

56 inquiry, almost always failed to solve the crime. This section
of the book is difficult to read, in a double sense: Its monotony
repels attention, and its subject—the rape, torture, and murder
of women and girls—repels imagination. In this way, Bolaño
enacts, and even makes the reader complicit in, the psychological mechanism that allows Santa Teresa to go on ignoring the
murders, even as they grow into a terrifying epidemic. The fact
that these killings are based on the real-life violence in Ciudad
Juarez—where, between 1993 and 2005, an estimated 370
women were murdered—adds a terrible irony to Bolaño's project. For most of us, these real-world murders are exactly what
history was to Aomame—a news item, briefly registered and
then ignored. It is only by means of fiction that we are compelled
to recognize their reality. Global fiction, in this case, is a tool for
undoing the complacency of global citizenship—a way of forcing
the reader to attend to the realities of the world's violence and
injustice.

Much of the force of the "The Part about the Crimes" comes
from the way it eschews the style—intensely poetic, surreal,
and digressive—that dominates 2666 and gives the book its
mysterious mood. The murders in Santa Teresa are the indi-
gestible core of reality, which can only be reported or recited.
Yet around that core, Bolaño weaves a richly unsettling universe
of images and stories—as if every aspect of the imagination is
commanded by, or serves to reflect, the corruption at the center. The key narrative technique of 2666 is digression: The
ostensible plot of each section is constantly being interrupted
by anecdotes, stories told by minor characters, things read in
books, and especially accounts of dreams. Dreams, suggests

one character—a man in prison in Santa Teresa who is a murder
suspect—are not isolated but shared, and they reflect a deeper
reality: "It's like a noise you hear in a dream. The dream, like
everything dreamed in enclosed spaces, is contagious. Suddenly
someone dreams it and after a while half the prisoners dream
it. But the *noise* you hear isn't part of the dream, it's real. The
noise belongs to a separate order of things." In a similar way, all
the proliferating narratives in 2666 are trying to communicate
a message from the heart of reality—a message that has to do
with violence and death.

The transitions between these miniature stories, these tiles
in the book's mosaic, are abrupt and unaccountable, giving the
sense that the book is proliferating almost beyond its author's
control. These are stories that seem to press forward, wanting
to tell themselves. Fittingly, then, nearly all the major characters
in the book turn out to be writers of one kind or another—that
is, professional tellers of stories. From the literary critics to the
reporter Oscar Fate to the novelist Archimboldi—whose biog-
raphy and connection with Santa Teresa are finally revealed in
the fifth section, "The Part about Archimboldi"—Bolaño creates a series of opportunities to reflect on different kinds of
writing.

Naturally, it is Archimboldi the novelist who is first in
rank among these writers, and who seems to come closest to
the mystery that defines the cosmos of 2666. Archimboldi, we
learn, is the pen name of Hans Reiter, a German World War II
veteran whose horrific experiences turned him into a vagrant
and misanthrope. Having lived through Europe's own "crimes,"
Bolaño implies, is what allows Archimboldi to become a great

58   imaginative writer—as opposed to the other writers in the
     book, who are mere craftsmen or critics. Perhaps different parts
     of the globe take turns as the point in closest contact with real-
     ity, as the winds of violence and chaos sweep over them. The
     key to literary creation, Bolaño's life and novel suggest, might
     be to remain in contact with that overwhelming reality, while
     retreating in space and in thought to the distance necessary for
     imaginative creation. If this feat involves a pressure of contra-
     diction that leads to deformity, even madness, then the book of
     our times must be mad—as 2666, with its bizarre beauty and
     force, insists on being.

To America and Back: Chimamanda Ngozi Adichie's *Americanah* and Mohsin Hamid's *The Reluctant Fundamentalist*

In the twentieth century, the immigrant experience was one of the most fruitful subjects for American fiction, with writers of many backgrounds exploring the always-relevant subject of what is gained and lost when people turn themselves into Americans. Today, immigrant experiences remain at the center of American letters—just witness the popularity and critical success of writers like Jhumpa Lahiri, whose work centers on Bengali immigrants, and Junot Diaz, who writes about Dominican-Americans. Yet immigration means something different today, in the age of the Internet and cheap jet travel, than it did in the era of Ellis Island. Globalization has brought with it the possibility of a new kind of life across borders, in which Americanness is not a replacement for one's original identity, but an added possibility in a repertoire of self-definitions.

Inevitably, a new genre of English-language fiction has
arisen to chronicle this experience: call it migrant literature,
rather than the more familiar term immigrant literature. Migrant
novels focus on characters for whom America is a stage of life
rather than a final destination. Their protagonists may come to
the First World legally or illegally, from a position of strength
or weakness. But they see life in America, and often Europe, as
means to an end—education, wealth, political freedom—rather
than ends in themselves. Because they often come from post-
colonial countries where English is already spoken, they don't
have to sacrifice their native language in order to function in the
First World. As a result, they are able to view the First World
from a critical perspective made possible by contrast and the
availability of other options. The migrant novel may turn out to
be one of the most significant literary expressions of the twenty-
first century, the portrait of an age when more and more people
have the ability to cross borders in both directions.

Americanah, the 2013 novel by Chimamanda Ngozi Adichie,
is already a classic of this new genre. Its title neatly captures its
double perspective on the United States: this is a book about
being American, like so many immigrant novels, yet the term
"Americanah" belongs to Nigerian English. It is used in the book
as a term of gentle mockery for Nigerians who live in the U.S. and
then return home, with new accents and affectations. Adichie's
perspective, then, will be emphatically that of an African on
America. Indeed, she proves that this point of view, both inside
and outside of both cultures, is an ideal one for a novelist, allowing her to see the complexities, absurdities, and hypocrisies of
both Nigerian and American society with a fresh eye. The novel

as a genre has always thrived on just the kind of social mobility,   63
and the corresponding confusion in social codes, which today
often takes place across national borders.

Adichie draws on her own experiences to tell the story of
Ifemelu, a Nigerian woman who arrives in the U.S. as a student
in the 1990s, and remains in the country until after the election
of Barack Obama in 2008. Yet as the book opens, we see Ifemelu
preparing to return home to Lagos; from the beginning, we
know that her time in America, which began as open-ended and
possibly permanent, has turned out to be only a sojourn. The
force that is calling her to return is primarily romantic: Despite
their long separation, she has never forgotten her first love,
Obinze, whose own experiences as a migrant in Britain form
one of the book's subplots. But it is clear that Ifemelu couldn't
return to Nigeria in the way she does—confidently, in possession of money, an American passport, and a successful career
as a blogger—if it hadn't been for her American experiences.
America, for her, has been a place to learn and grow, but never a
permanent home: "Nigeria became where she was supposed to
be, the only place she could sink her roots in without the constant urge to tug them out and shake off the soil."

The classic novel of manners is a bourgeois genre, plotting
the way money and love intersect for people who are in possession of at least some of each. *Americanah* belongs in this
tradition, with the twist that it maps class and romance onto
the wider and more directly political terrain of nation and race.
Ifemelu and Obinze, who meet as teenage students in Lagos,
both belong to Nigeria's frustrated middle class. Their parents
are civil servants whose potential for advancement has been

64   blocked by a sclerotic and corrupt society and state. Ifemelu's
     father loses his job in a government agency when he refuses
     to address his boss obsequiously as "Mummy," and Obinze's
     mother is a professor whose university is chronically under-
     funded and on strike.

     These young people are by no means destitute—their lives
     are immune from war and want, unlike those of Nigerians of a
     different class or an earlier generation. Yet they are afflicted by
     a sense of stasis, the impossibility of advancing individually or
     nationally. At a dinner party with white Britons, Obinze reflects
     that First World liberals "understood the fleeing from war, from
     the kind of poverty that crushed human souls, but they would
     not understand the need to escape from the oppressive leth-
     argy of choicelessness." This choicelessness means that young
     Nigerians are drawn, inevitably, to life abroad. Adichie shows
     that the choice of whether to aspire to a life in America or in
     Britain is one of the key dividing lines in their circle of friends.
     People who vacation abroad, and come home bearing Western
     goods or speaking foreign slang, enjoy an intangible prestige.
     Adichie does not depict the furious envy and resentment of the
     West characteristic of an earlier generation of post-colonial
     writers, but rather a kind of fashionable longing, which she sees
     as a foible more than a vice.

     From this starting point in the middle-middle class, both
     Ifemelu and Obinze make their way into Nigeria's elite, but by very
     different routes. From the beginning, Adichie shows that the fate
     of a migrant is largely in the hands of luck, starting with the luck
     of receiving a visa. Ifemelu, who gets a student visa to the U.S., is
     launched onto a path of academic and professional respectability;

Obinze, who slips into the U.K. without a visa, is an illegal alien
in constant fear of the police. This is not to say that Ifemelu's
path is entirely smooth. Because she has no money and her visa
doesn't allow her to work, she is forced into the underground
economy, reaching her lowest point when she engages in a single
act of sex work. This experience traumatizes her and sends her
into a depression, while also alienating her from Obinze, who cannot understand her sudden silence and refusal to answer emails or
phone calls.

Love, luck, and money are all chance variables in the equa-
tion that spells success or failure for the immigrant. This
becomes even clearer when Adichie tells the story of Obinze
in England, whose friends fail to help him get a good job, and
who is reduced to paying a stranger for a green card marriage. It is just before this marriage is to be finalized that he is
arrested and deported, possibly betrayed by one of the preda-
tory marriage-brokers who arranged it. But if these perversions
of love threaten to destroy Adichie's characters, Ifemelu is
saved by genuine love. Thanks to loyal Nigerian friends, she
is able to find an under-the-counter babysitting job; through
this job, she meets Curt, an American who falls in love with
her and helps her get an office position with a green card.
While Ifemelu is never portrayed as using these relationships
transactionally—Adichie insists on keeping her a fully sympathetic heroine—the novel makes clear that she would not have
thrived in America were it not for Curt, a man whose affection
she reciprocates even though she never fully respects him.

Curt is emblematic of one of Adichie's favorite satirical
themes: the complacent hypocrisy of white Americans about

66 race. Ifemelu seldom encounters institutional or violent racism in the United States, but she is constantly running up against the unspoken rules and expectations of both whites and blacks. Often Adichie plays these for comedy, especially when she is writing about the efforts of American whites to bend over backward to prove that they don't recognize race at all, even though it is constantly on their minds. In one scene, Ifemelu is shopping at a store where there are two clerks, one white and one black. When the cashier is trying to figure out which clerk has helped her, she asks Ifemelu to identify them by the length of their hair or other markers, but refuses to simply ask if it was the white or the black woman—and finally gives up rather than bring race into the conversation.

The repository for Ifemelu's observations on race is her blog, "Raceteenth or Various Observations about American Blacks (Those Formerly Known as Negroes) by a Non-American Black." Adichie gives a number of examples of these blog posts, such as one in which Ifemelu jokes that "in America, racism exists but racists are all gone." It is this false consciousness about racism that prevents Curt, and other well-meaning white people, from fully understanding Ifemelu's experiences in American society. She herself has to work hard to understand race, since it is only once she arrives in America that she becomes conscious of herself as the bearer of a racialized identity. One of the sites of that identity is apparently trivial, but conceals interesting depths: hair. Several scenes in the novel take place in a braiding salon, where Ifemelu is both drawn to and alienated from the African hairdressers; and Adichie writes bitterly about the pressure on black women to relax their natural hair. Hair is one of those

silent signifiers of race, class, and nation that is particularly
available for a novelist like Adichie, who is constantly observing
the gulf between what people say and what they mean.

By the end of the novel, Adichie has brought both Obinze
and Ifemelu back to Lagos, where they are able to overcome the
last obstacles to their reunion. Ifemelu has become a chroni-
cler of the city's social elite, particularly former expatriates like
herself, whose foreign fads—like vegetarianism—she affec-
tionately lampoons. Obinze, meanwhile, has become very rich,
thanks to his new status as the protege of one of Nigeria's well-
connected "Big Men." Both are beneficiaries of the country's
growing middle class, whose ostentatious displays of wealth are
made possible, they fully recognize, by deep-seated corruption
and inequality. In a sense, then, their happy ending is a fluke, in
a country still plagued by violence, exploitation, and religious
discord. The global economy has advantaged them individu-
ally, even as it continues to wreak havoc on Nigeria as a whole.
(Adichie gets in a sharp critique of the Western oil companies
that extract the country's resources while giving little in return.)

But in general, Adichie writes about this state of affairs
with less indignation than fascination. The genre of the novel,
Americanah reminds us, has always thrived by chronicling
upwardly mobile people, and the means of that mobility is seldom pure—just look at Balzac, or Henry James. Indeed, the
clash of cultures and classes which globalization brings with it
is creating fertile ground for the traditional novel. This is particularly true of the Anglophone novel, which can speak easily
across national boundaries, and has a rich history of social comedy to draw on. The absence of overt politics in *Americanah* does

68   not mean that Adichie is an apolitical writer; only that, like the
classic novelists of manners, she sees the way people love, dress,
and make their living as themselves inherently political.

It is possible to imagine Changez, the narrator of Mohsin
Hamid's *The Reluctant Fundamentalist* (2007), crossing paths
with Ifemelu—perhaps at Princeton, where he is an under-
graduate and she spends a year on a fellowship. But while
Adichie's heroine struggles with poverty and only succeeds in
America through some turns of good luck, Hamid's protagonist
is a gilded youth, for whom success in the New World seems
assured. From the moment he leaves Pakistan for a full scholarship in the Ivy League, Changez is riding on the escalator of
global capitalism to its giddy heights: a job in finance, a rich sal-
ary, world travel. He even wins the love of an Upper East Side
princess, symbolizing his fairy-tale conquest of a kingdom that
is, in Hamid's telling, there for the taking by the ambitious and
talented immigrant.

At the highest levels of the meritocracy, Changez reflects,
even race and religion present no real divisions. Looking at
his fellow new employees at Underwood Samson, a consulting firm, he observes: "Two of my five colleagues were women;
Wainwright and I were non-white. We were marvelously
diverse ... and yet we were not: All of us ... hailed from the same
elite universities—Harvard, Princeton, Stanford, Yale; we all
exuded a sense of confident self-satisfaction; and not one of us
was either short or overweight." Here we see America inheriting
one of the traditional strengths of empire—its ability to recruit
its personnel from all its provinces, yet mold them in the image

and values of the center. Tellingly, Changez goes on to reflect
that "shorn of hair and dressed in battle fatigues, we would have
been virtually indistinguishable." For while these management
consultants never pick up a gun, they are, in Hamid's vision,
a kind of praetorian guard for the American empire. Their job
involves flying to cities around the world—generally places
much poorer than New York—and telling the natives how to
conduct their business.

Yet when we first meet Changez, he is no longer a New
Yorker: The immigrant, it turns out, was really a migrant all
along. The framing device of the novel is an encounter between
him, as the book's narrator, and an unnamed, unspeaking
American interlocutor, who has come to find him in a market
in Lahore. This American, we quickly learn from Changez's
cutting and freighted observations, is heavily muscled, highly
nervous, and armed; in short, we conclude, he is a soldier or CIA
agent, whose mission may well be to kill our charming narrator.
This narrative structure, with its echoes of Conrad's *Heart of
Darkness* and Camus's *The Fall*, is designed to keep the reader
constantly unsettled, waiting for the promised violence to
erupt—and striving to figure out how Changez became enough
of a threat to warrant a possible assassination.

To reject America and go back home is, for Ifemelu, a per-
sonal choice with political overtones; for Changez it is a directly
political decision, one that he takes at the risk of his life. What
accounts for the difference between these migrant stories?
Gender, religion, and nationality all play a role: As a Pakistani
Muslim man, Changez finds himself in a very different relationship to America than does Ifemelu, a Nigerian Christian woman.

70   This is especially true after the attacks of September 11, which take place just a few months into his tenure at Underwood Samson. All along, Changez has been acutely aware of the differences between himself and his American classmates and workmates. Their nonchalant sense of privilege, their casual wealth, regularly grate on him.

But it is not until he sees the Twin Towers fall, on television, that Changez fully realizes how much resentment he has accumulated toward the empire he is serving. His first reaction, he confesses, was to smile: "Yes, despicable as it may sound, my initial reaction was to be remarkably pleased. . . . I was caught up in the *symbolism* of it all, the fact that someone had so visibly brought America to her knees." Changez does not sympathize with the religious or political goals of al-Qaeda, which is never mentioned by name. Though a Muslim, he seems to live an entirely secular life, and he never really becomes the "fundamentalist" of the title. Rather, his resentment is rooted in a more general sense that, as a native of the Third World, his place is with the victims of American power rather than with its agents. The international popularity of *The Reluctant Fundamentalist*, which was translated into twenty-five languages and made into a film, suggests that this emotion has a global resonance.

This instinct makes his position as a consultant at Underwood Samson uncomfortable, and finally untenable. In a telling scene, Changez is riding through the streets of Manila, where he has been sent for work, in a limousine, when he makes eye contact with the driver of a jeepney, a kind of bus. "There was an undisguised hostility in his expression; I had no idea why . . . But his dislike was obvious, so *intimate*, that it got under

my skin." Suddenly he is struck by the fact that, physically and
biographically, he has much more in common with the Filipino
bus driver than he does with the white Americans riding with
him in the limousine. Eventually he begins to sabotage his work,
from an unspoken sense of solidarity with the people he is
meant to be "rationalizing" out of a job.

If *The Reluctant Fundamentalist* were only a story of rebellion and disaffection, however, it would be less true to the
real dynamics of American power, which can seduce as well as
impose. For Changez, this seduction takes place through the
person of Erica, whose heavily symbolic name ("I am Erica," she
could say) is an appropriate counterweight to Changez's own.
(Changez is a version of Genghis, the "backward" Mongol con-
queror who swept away the advanced empires of his own time.)
Hamid's most interesting and counterintuitive choice in the
novel is to make Erica, not a confident or spoiled exemplar of
American materialism, but a deeply damaged character. When
Changez meets her, on a summer trip after graduating from
Princeton, Erica is just barely recovered from the early death of
her childhood love, Chris. During their brief, hesitant court-
ship, Changez is never sure whether Erica is going to be able to
put Chris behind her and love again, or whether the trauma of
the loss will return, plunging her into depression and fantasy.
Finally, the lure of memory and fantasy turn out to be too great.
At the end of the novel Erica disappears from the asylum where
she has been recuperating, seemingly a suicide.

If, for Changez at any rate, Erica represents America, the
allegory turns out to be a provocative one. Publicly, the country's response to the trauma of 9/11 might seem strong and

72   active, even to excess—prosecuting the war on terror, invad-
ing Afghanistan and Iraq. But Hamid sees this aggression as a
symptom of a country retreating into a nostalgic fantasy, com-
forting itself with stories of a simpler past—just as Erica finds it
easier to remember Chris than to engage with Changez. Hamid
makes the parallel explicit: "What your fellow countrymen
longed for was unclear to me—a time of unquestioned domi-
nance? of safety? of moral uncertainty? I did not know—but
that they were scrambling to don the costumes of another era
was apparent. I felt treacherous for wondering whether that era
was fictitious, and whether—if it could indeed be animated—it
contained a part written for someone like me."

    Finally, when Changez returns home for a visit to a Pakistan
on the brink of war with India—a war that, unfairly perhaps, he
sees the United States as permitting or encouraging—he realizes that his place is in the country of his birth, not the empire
that offers to adopt him. The global order, Hamid suggests, may
appear to be a truly international meritocracy, in which the
most talented people of all nations can rise to the top. But in
fact, globalization serves as a cover for American domination,
so that serving it, for a non-American, inevitably involves a sacrifice of self-respect. Rather than accept this Faustian bargain,
Changez returns to Lahore and becomes a university lecturer,
popular among the students for his vocal anti-Americanism. It
is this political stance that has brought him to the attention of
the mysterious American, to whom he spends the whole book
explaining and justifying himself. For the irony of rebellion is
that it makes the rebel subservient to what he rebels against. If

Changez's migrant experience has turned him against America,
it is still America which dominates his imagination of power
and injustice. In this way, the migrant's experience of America,
be it friendly or hostile, serves as a route to the creation of a
global political consciousness.

Fearful Futures: Margaret Atwood's *Oryx and Crake* and Michel Houellebecq's *The Possibility of an Island*

If world literature is an arena of struggle, as Casanova and other observers insist, it is not just a struggle for fame or prestige. What is at stake in the idea of the global novel is authority: Who has the right to represent the world in fiction? Most writers, of course, would shy away from staking their claim in such large terms. The novel does not usually attempt to depict or pronounce upon the entire world at once. Rather, it offers a record of how people in a particular time and place imagine, and negotiate, their place in the world. But there is one kind of fiction which, necessarily, involves the author in making forecasts and judgments, not about one country or culture, but about humanity as a whole. That is the fiction of global apocalypse—novels that imagine the disappearance of civilization, or even of the human race itself.

Ever since H. G. Wells's *The Time Machine*, this sort of speculative tale has perched on the border between science fiction and literary fiction. But in the twenty-first century, the idea of the radical decline or annihilation of humanity has become increasingly salient for serious literature, as the specter of nuclear war has been replaced in our nightmares by the prospect of environmental catastrophe. The greatest dystopian novels have always been reflections of the societies that produced them, using then-cutting-edge scientific metaphors to indict present social ills. Wells's Morlocks and Eloi are a Darwinian parable about class conflict; Aldous Huxley's *Brave New World* depicts a philistine mass society created through behavioral conditioning; and George Orwell's *1984* imagines the coupling of surveillance technology with ideological indoctrination.

Two of the most important apocalyptic novels of the early twenty-first century, *Oryx and Crake* by Margaret Atwood (2003) and *The Possibility of an Island* by Michel Houellebecq (2005), follow in this same tradition. Indeed, though writers more different than Atwood and Houellebecq can hardly be imagined—the Canadian feminist and the French misogynist—their prophecies converge in remarkable ways. Both books imagine a future in which humanity has been not just extinguished by its own environmental recklessness, but also superseded by a genetically engineered race of quasi-human creatures. They imagine human beings as sorcerers' apprentices, heedlessly summoning the forces that will destroy them; and they pose the question of whether such a denouement to the human story might be well-deserved. After all, if humanity has proved to be such a reckless

78   steward of the Earth, perhaps some new species ought to have a
      chance.

      This is global fiction in the most emphatic sense, pass-
ing judgment on humanity as such and on the world order
it has created. Yet to read Atwood and Houellebecq is to
encounter the difficulty, narrative and moral, of such a universal judgment. For inevitably, their diagnoses of the state of
twenty-first-century humanity originate in their experience of
particular societies—both of them advanced Western countries. Indeed, *Oryx and Crake* and *The Possibility of an Island* can
be read as commentaries on the malaise that accompanies late
capitalism—conditions that do not apply in most of the world,
however acute they may be from the vantage point of North
America and Western Europe. To predict, and in some sense to
endorse, the destruction of humanity because of the ailments
of rich Western societies might well seem like an imperialism
of the imagination, using the entire globe as a stage on which to
enact "First World Problems."

      In particular, for both novelists it is the sexual unhappi-
ness of Western societies that sounds the alarm on a sinking
ship. Both Jimmy, the central character in *Oryx and Crake*, and
Daniel, the narrator of *The Possibility of an Island*, serve as prime
exhibits in an indictment of modern male sexuality. Jimmy,
whose adolescence and young adulthood are narrated in one of
Atwood's alternating time-frames, is a depressive seducer, who
parades his emotional scars—he was abandoned in childhood
by his mother—in order to win the sympathy of sensitive, artistic women. "They saw him as a creative project," Atwood writes:
"the raw material, Jimmy in his present gloomy form; the end

product, a happy Jimmy." But Jimmy has no intention of being
healed by any of the women he sleeps with. His relationships
follow a standard pattern of seduction and withdrawal, ending
in his "being dumped, even though he himself had maneuvered
the event into place." Less an outright villain than a selfish
adolescent, Jimmy is Atwood's portrait of a prevailing stunted
masculinity: "He really did love these women, sort of. . . . It was
just that he had a short attention span."

The flip side of Jimmy's small-scale exploitation of women
is the horrific trade in female bodies, for purposes of rape and
pornography, that forms another major plot strand in *Oryx
and Crake*. Here the key character is the woman known only as
Oryx—a code-name assigned her by Crake, the novel's sinister
genetic-engineering mastermind, who himself was originally
called Glenn. Glenn was Jimmy's childhood friend, and Jimmy's
role in the novel is to serve as witness to Glenn's increasingly
hubristic experiments for the "improvement," and finally the
replacement, of human beings. For Glenn, the adoption of an
exotic animal nickname is a way of paying homage to extinct
species, and of signaling his alienation from humanity, which
soon will take the same path to extinction.

But for Oryx, namelessness goes deeper: the reader never
learns her true name, even as Atwood relates her nightmare
childhood in a Third World country (also unnamed). As a child,
she is sold into slavery by her poor parents, and soon handed
over to a human trafficker who uses her for prostitution and
forces her to act in pornographic videos. It is in one of these videos that the teenage Jimmy first glimpses her, and is struck with
a combination of love and horror that never leaves him: "Jimmy

80 felt burned by this look—eaten into, as if by acid . . . for the first time he'd felt that what they'd been doing was wrong. Before, it had always been entertainment, or else far beyond his control, but now he felt culpable."

When Jimmy reencounters Oryx—or at least, the woman he believes to be the girl from the video—in real life, he falls in love with her. But Atwood deliberately keeps Oryx's own consciousness veiled from the reader. Like Jimmy, we are viewing her, not really understanding her. As a result, we can never be sure whether her relationship with Jimmy, or with any man, could ever be more to Oryx than just another form of exploitation. Is there a difference between staged rape and real lovemaking? "He never did anything with me that you don't do," Oryx tells Jimmy, referring to her captor and rapist. "I don't do them against your will," Jimmy objects, but Oryx merely laughs: "What is my will?" she answers. Neither Jimmy nor the reader is ever sure, and so Oryx becomes a living symbol of the inscrutable exploitativeness of all sexuality—at least, all male sexuality.

And if this is so, if sexuality is inherently corrupt, then perhaps the world would be better off without it. That is the belief of Crake, who from the beginning has an Asperger's-like indifference to all human relationships, especially sexual ones. Eventually, he rises to become the chief genetic engineer of a company called RejoovenEsense (illiterate spelling is one of the minor features of Atwood's dystopia), which is trying to find a "cure" for mortality itself. In this role Crake creates a small number of prototypes of a posthuman species, which Jimmy names "Crakers," who lack the most egregious types of human frailty. A prime example of the way the Crakers improve on humanity, in ways that seem to betray basic human values, is that they are designed to eat their own excrement. Since they are grass-grazing herbivores, like cows, this allows them to extract more nutrients from food; but it also violates one of the most primal human taboos.

So, too, with Craker sexuality. The mating ritual of the Crakers is utilitarian: when a female is in heat, the males perform a mating dance, and she picks four men to take turns having intercourse with her. This eliminates the possibility of coercion—the woman remains in control of when and with whom she has sex—and also blurs paternity, so that the Crakers can have no concept of nuclear families or inherited property. In this way, Crake does away with what he sees as the irrational and destructive elements in sex: "No more No means yes anyway. . . . No more prostitution, no sexual abuse of children, no haggling over the price, no pimps, no sex slaves. No more rape." Yet these same elements are also, Atwood suggests, the ones that allow for sex to be the site of mystery, intimacy, even holiness. As Jimmy reflects, there is "no more unrequited love these days, no more thwarted lust; no more shadow between the desire and the act."

In this way, Atwood's dystopia mirrors that of Huxley, who also recoiled from a future in which sex would be stripped of any sense of mystery. But while *Brave New World* was fairly unambiguous in its negative judgment on the future it imagined, *Oryx and Crake* remains stubbornly undecided. The novel takes place in two time-frames: its "past" is sometime in our medium-term future, perhaps towards the end of this century, while its "present" takes place in the immediate aftermath of a

82 global plague, launched deliberately by Crake, that has annihi-
lated almost all human beings. Before the disaster, Jimmy is a
fairly ordinary man; after, he becomes "Snowman," a mythical
creature in the minds of the Crakers, who represent the future
masters of the planet.

Central to the novel's effect is that, even before the plague
breaks out, human beings are shown to have wrought terrible
damage on the earth and on their own societies. Jimmy grows
up in what seems to be the United States, but it is a country
seemingly without a government, divided between corporate-
owned "compounds," where some semblance of middle-class
security remains, and the wild "pleeblands," where crime and
chaos reign. This is a world of devastating heat and storms, in
which almost all the food is made of soy, presumably because
animals have gone extinct. Meanwhile, high culture seems
to have disappeared. One of Atwood's bitter jokes is directed
against higher education: in this future, only the worst students are tracked into the humanities, where they are prepared
for jobs churning out ad copy. Good students, like Crake, are
recruited like athletes to the best, corporate-owned schools,
where they become scientific masters of the universe.

Things are so bad, in Atwood's imagined future, that the
reader feels a pull of sympathy with Crake's sociopathic urge to
destroy everything and start over. For there is an unmistakable
parallel between the victimization of Oryx and the victimization of the planet itself: both are the result of innate, insatiable
human greed. "Human society," according to one of Jimmy's
pre-catastrophe acquaintances, "was a sort of monster, its main
by-products being corpses and rubble. It never learned, it made

the same cretinous mistakes over and over, trading short-term gain for long-term pain. It was like a giant slug eating its way relentlessly through all the other bioforms on the planet, grinding up life on earth and shitting it out the backside in the form of pieces of manufactured soon-to-be-obsolete plastic junk."

So comprehensive is the novel's indictment of humanity that, in its final scene—when Jimmy-turned-Snowman discovers that he is not, after all, the sole human survivor—the reader is left uncertain whether the survival of other people is a good thing or a curse. Snowman himself must decide whether to protect the Crakers by killing these human interlopers, thus effectively completing Crake's own genocide. Does humanity deserve to live? The novel ends on that cliff-hanging question, but the fact that Atwood could make the reader's answer so uncertain—overriding our natural instincts in favor of human survival—is a testament to the power of her apocalyptic diagnosis. What distinguishes twenty-first-century dystopian fiction from its forerunners is that, unlike with Orwell or Huxley, we remain uncertain whether the coming disaster ought to be averted.

When it comes to sexuality, Daniel, the narrator of *The Possibility of an Island*, makes Jimmy look wholesome and well-adjusted. Not unlike his creator, Michel Houellebecq, Daniel is a professional provocateur—a stand-up comedian and filmmaker whose stock-in-trade is graphic violence, insult, and pornography. One of his films is described as featuring fifteen minutes' worth of "the unremitting explosion of babies' skulls under the impact of shots from a high-caliber revolver." His anti-Arab

84 show *We Prefer the Palestinian Orgy Sluts* is balanced by an anti-Semitic sequel, *Munch on My Gaza Strip (My Huge Jewish Settler)*. But if Daniel is grotesque, he is less grotesque than the audience that adores him, making him a rich European celebrity. Like Atwood with her compounds and pleeblands, Houellebecq seizes on disquieting features of our world—in this case, an increasingly vulgar culture—and accelerates them, forcing us to recognize ourselves in a distorting mirror.

As Daniel narrates his life in twenty-first-century France, however, it becomes clear that the violence and despair which animate his comedy are destroying his soul. Sex, for Houellebecq as for Atwood, is the arena in which the spiritual decay of contemporary Western society is most obvious. Daniel is fixated on the idea that "sexual pleasure was . . . superior, in refinement and violence, to all the other pleasures life had to offer." In a society devoted to consumption, sexual consumption is the acme of human activity, the thing that makes life worth living. But he is relentlessly aware of the fact that sexual desirability declines with age: "Youth was the time for happiness, its only season," he reflects. "The physical bodies of young people [are] the only desirable possession the world has ever produced." Living by this maxim, Daniel must also fall by it. First he leaves his wife when she becomes middle-aged and her body stops pleasing him; then he is left by his much younger girlfriend, who sees him as too old to be fully human.

Despite his many graphic descriptions of sex, however, Houellebecq is finally not a pornographer but a moralist. He leaves no doubt that, in the absence of any values beyond immediate pleasure, life is intolerable. By the end of the

book Daniel is reduced to a near-zombie, whose only worldly
attachment is to his dog. Like the European society whose
perfect product he is, Daniel is spiritually sick unto death, in
dire need of a reason to keep living. And it is just this reason
which he, and the world, discover in the most unlikely place: a
crackpot cult known as the Elohimites. This group, unmistak-
ably based on the real-life cult known as the Raelians, believes
that humanity is the creation of alien intelligences, who will
one day return to Earth to sort out its problems. In the mean-
time, the Elohimites, from their base on the Atlantic island of
Lanzarote, are using cutting-edge scientific research to find a
way to eliminate death.

Like Crake in Atwood's novel, however, the mad scien-
tist in *The Possibility of an Island*—whom Daniel nicknames
"Knowall"—can only abolish death by abolishing human nature
with it. We know that this quest will succeed because this novel,
too, is narrated in two time frames: The near-present experience of "Daniel1," as he is called, alternates with the far-future
reflections of his clones, Daniel24 and Daniel25. These descen-
dants of Daniel are what are known as "neohumans," products of
the cloning and genetic engineering process that the Elohimites
created. Like the Crakers, they have left behind the most nox-
ious features of human beings—their sexual drives, their need
for excretion, their waywardness and unhappiness. In fact, the
neohumans have totally withdrawn from the world; they live
from birth to death in separate apartments, meeting their own
kind only through computer screens. This seclusion allows the
neohumans to survive the series of wars and environmental
catastrophes that, we gradually learn, have virtually eliminated

86   the human race, leaving only a few bands of roaming "savages" to
      inhabit a transformed planet.

      In much the same way as Atwood, Houellebecq structures
his novel around the question of whether this future is truly
dystopian, or whether it might represent a kind of rough justice.
After all, the novel's main specimen of present-day humanity is
Daniel, a thoroughly selfish, loathsome, and miserable person.
And Houellebecq insists that it is the logic of human existence
that made him that way. We are condemned, in our current
incarnation, to the cruelty of desire and the emptiness of consumption, the need for sex and the dread of age. Like Jimmy in
Oryx and Crake, Daniel is faced with a symbolic choice in which
he must pass judgment on the worthiness of human beings to
survive.

      At a crucial moment in the emergence of the Elohimite cult,
its prophet is murdered, and the surviving leaders conspire to
put forward the prophet's son as his literal reincarnation—the
prophet's mind transplanted into a new body. For the trick to
work, however, an innocent witness to the murder must be done
away with. Is there anything inherently sacred about human life,
or does it deserve to disappear to make way for the new? "What
[Knowall] was trying to do," Daniel realizes, "was create a new
species, which would have no more moral obligation toward
humans that the humans had toward jellyfish or lizards; I real-
ized, above all, that I would have no scruples about belonging to
this new species, that my disgust at murder was of a sentimen-
tal or emotional, rather than a rational, nature."

      By acquiescing in the murder of the witness, Daniel wins
the eternal life he hoped for. He becomes an Elohimite, indeed a

kind of apostle of the new faith, and his life story is studied by
his clones for centuries into the future, just as Christians read
the Gospels. But Houellebecq complicates the moral stakes in
The Possibility of an Island by subtly portraying the future state
inhabited by Daniel25 as anything but paradisal. By eliminat-
ing the evils of human nature, the neohumans have also lost the
ambition, curiosity, and love of life that make life worth living
in the first place. Notably, they have lost all interest in scientific
progress: "Since the Standard Genetic Rectification . . . no mod-
ification of any real significance has been developed," Daniel25
notes. As a clone, he is required to spend his time reading the
autobiography of Daniel1, which is the narrative the reader has
also been following. Nominally this is so that the later iteration of Daniel can better incarnate the original; but it is also,
Houellebecq suggests, because the last human generation was
the last generation interesting enough to read about. In this way,
Houellebecq makes literature itself party to his indictment of
humanity. Our desire for interesting stories makes us complicit
in the survival of a corrupt human race.

Houellebecq shares with Atwood a certainty that the state
of the world he deplores is traceable to permanently objec-
tionable features of human nature. "The root of all evil was
biological and independent of any imaginable social transformation," Daniel insists. Indeed, both novelists, in their fatalism
about humanity, are profoundly anti-political. Products of a
post-Cold War world, they have definitely abandoned any faith
in the idea of revolution—the messianic transformation of
society that for generations ensured a margin of social hope.
Today, when we think about the future, we think of biological

88   laws rather than political options. We are no longer Hegelian
      creatures of History, but Darwinian competitors, living out
      the iron rule of survival of the fittest. If humanity perishes,
      both Atwood and Houellebecq suggest, it is because the spe-
      cies is no longer fit, either practically or morally, to sustain its
      predominance.

      But it is unmistakable that this form of globalism—this
      way of pronouncing imaginatively on the worth of the entire
      human species and the prospects for its future—is based pri-
      marily on the experience of modern Western societies. Atwood
      depicts a world in which unfettered capitalism has destroyed
      both society and nature; Houellebecq depicts a world in which
      that same capitalism has eroded human ties and created a soci-
      ety of atomized, alienated individuals. But in chronicling the
      discontents of abundance and freedom, these writers have little
      to say about the greater portion of the globe, where abundance
      and freedom remain utopian ideals. By imaginatively putting
      an end to humanity, these novels preclude the possibility that
      other places can share in the West's blessings, and possibly put
      them to better use.

      Indeed, there is an implication in this apocalyptic fiction
      that the West is the end state for all humanity, or the avant-
      garde of human progress: Where the West leads, the rest will
      inevitably follow. (Houellebecq suggests as much when he
      anticipates the mass conversion of Islamic societies, as well as
      Christian ones, to Elohimism.) On this assumption, it makes
      sense that the despair of the West should generate despair
      about the whole world. But this conflation of the current

historical experience of the West with the essence and fate of   89
humankind is itself a kind of colonialism. Here lies one of the
deepest temptations of the global novel: In drawing a portrait
of the world, a writer may, perhaps must, end up producing
only a self-portrait.

Starting from Home: Elena Ferrante's Neapolitan Novels

The critics of "world literature" envision the global literary ecosystem as being similar to, because it is a part of, the global system of capital. Attacks on world literature often read like attacks on globalization itself, with each economic sin fostering a parallel literary sin. Just as the global economy concentrates power and wealth in the hands of a few while impoverishing the many, so world literature grants disproportionate fame and readership to a handful of world-famous writers, while consigning the majority to obscurity, regardless of merit. Global capitalism rewards standardization and consistency of products, from hamburgers to cellphones; world literature produces a similar standardization of style, flattening idiosyncrasies and favoring an easily consumable style, preferably in English. Each part of the literary indictment seems plausible precisely because its charges are familiar from the broader discourse of anti-globalization.

Yet if the critical consensus against world literature were correct, there would be no way to explain the emergence of a writer like Elena Ferrante. In the last five years, no writer has risen more rapidly to world fame than Ferrante, mainly on the strength of her "Neapolitan novels," a series of four books published in English between 2012 and 2015: *My Brilliant Friend*, *The Story of a New Name*, *Those Who Leave and Those Who Stay*, and *The Story of the Lost Child*. Before the first novel in the series appeared, Ferrante was barely known outside of Italy. Now her books are international bestsellers, and are scheduled for publication in dozens of languages from Chinese to Hebrew. In 2016 she was named one of *Time* magazine's 100 Most Influential People, a sign that her reputation has expanded beyond the literary world and entered the mass media. In Ferrante's case, the process Casanova illuminates—of discovery, critical legitimation, translation, and canonization—has taken place almost overnight. This suggests that her work answers immediately and profoundly to critics' and readers' expectations of what novels should be.

Yet Ferrante and her work are, in every way, the opposite of what critics of "world literature" decry. The Neapolitan novels are not thinly generic but richly particular; not international in scope but localized, on the scale of a single neighborhood; not about isolated individuals traveling through a featureless world, but about the thick web of social and economic relationships that determine the course of individual lives. Nor does Ferrante herself participate in the media and publicity processes that turn writers into commodities. Rather, "Elena Ferrante" is a pen name for a writer whose true identity remains unknown, and

94   she has refused since the beginning of her career to make public
        appearances of any kind.

        Ferrante has described this anonymity as a principled
        attempt to return the focus of reading from the author-as-
        celebrity to the text itself. In the media, she complained to *The
        Paris Review*, "It's not the book that counts, but the aura of its
        author. If the aura is already there, and the media reinforces it,
        the publishing world is happy to open its doors and the mar-
        ket is very happy to welcome you. If it's not there but the book
        miraculously sells, the media invents the author, so the writer
        ends up selling not only his work but also himself, his image."
        Refusing to sell herself, however, has not injured Ferrante's
        commercial or critical prospects. On the contrary, it has fueled
        both curiosity and respect from her audience.

        Like traditional novelists of manners, Ferrante begins from
        the assumption that the most important factors shaping indi-
        vidual destinies are local. The Neapolitan novels tell the story
        of two women, Elena Greco and Rafaella "Lila" Cerullo, whose
        entire lives are determined by and even prefigured in their earli-
        est experiences of family, neighborhood, and school. Over the
        course of the four books, Lila never leaves Naples, while Elena
        ends up returning to the city despite her strongest attempts to
        escape it. Notably, both of their lives are populated by the same
        cast of characters from the age of five to the age of sixty. The
        people of "the neighborhood," as Ferrante refers to the slum
        where they grow up, are forever turning up in new guises, like
        the characters in Proust.

        Yet the world in which these friends come to maturity is
        shaped by influences and experiences that are international:

the political and cultural turmoil of the 1960s, the rise of feminism in the 1970s, and the advent of information technology in the 1980s. In this sense, the Neapolitan novels tell an Italian story that might equally well be told of women of the same generation around the world. This is a story of emergence and of the failure to emerge—from scarcity to abundance, from tradition to autonomy, from the past to the future. Individual lives, Ferrante suggests, take place at the intersection of the local and the global, and are the product of their dialectic. Just as it is impossible to live an immediately global existence, untethered to language or place, so it is impossible to live an entirely local existence, uninfluenced by history, politics, and economics.

The inescapability of this dialectic is an ironic lesson that it takes Elena Greco, the novels' narrator, a lifetime to learn. When the series begins, in *My Brilliant Friend,* Elena seems to be on an upward trajectory out of the neighborhood, while Lila seems destined to be imprisoned there forever. The difference in their fates is owed entirely to the decisions of their fathers about whether the girls will be allowed to progress in their education beyond primary school. This is a concrete example of how patriarchy determines the course of women's lives, and Naples in the 1950s, when the main characters are children, is a patriarchy in the purest sense. Women live under the control of men, depend on the favor of men, and exist in constant fear of men. Domestic violence, sexual harassment, rape, and even murder are the common currency of life in the neighborhood.

For Ferrante, the backwardness and misery of this life are reflected in language—specifically, in the use of Neapolitan dialect, which throughout the series is a marker of class, education, and temperament. (Notably, this is a feature of the original that cannot easily be translated; Ferrante, clearly, is not concerned about making her style effortlessly consumable around the world.) Both Elena and Lila grow up speaking dialect, which Ferrante insistently portrays as a tongue made for obscenity and threat. But at school, Elena learns to speak and write proper Italian, an acquisition that begins her subtle alienation from her surroundings. It is her ability to learn, her exceptional diligence as a student, that offers Elena a ladder out of the neighborhood. Yet Lila, she insists from the beginning, is far more gifted than she is; if Elena is an A student, Lila is a genius. Indeed, throughout her life, whatever Lila turns her hand to is a triumph. We find her at various stages designing a shoe that becomes a bestseller, making a poster that is a stunning work of art, teaching herself to program early punch-card computers, and starting a successful business.

Because she was not allowed to continue in school, however, Lila never acquires the language—the Italian speech, but also the manners, habits, and expectations—needed to emancipate herself from the Neapolitan lower class. Elena, on the other hand, learns the habits of diligence, repression, and self-sacrifice needed to succeed at each stage of her education, until she finally wins a scholarship to study classics at the university of Pisa. The question that haunts the series is the one posed by the title of the first book: Which of these women is really the "brilliant friend"? To all appearances, it is Elena, who escapes the neighborhood, earns a prestigious degree, becomes a professional writer, and marries into a rich and influential family. Elena, however, is certain that the brilliant one is really

Lila, whose world remains confined to Naples, yet who rises
by the force of her personality and intelligence to a position of
supreme, almost mythic power in the neighborhood.

The different courses of the women's lives are encapsulated
in the title of the third book in the series, *Those Who Leave and
Those Who Stay*. They are prefigured in an important early episode, where Elena and Lila, as children, decide to "skip school,
and cross the boundaries of the neighborhood." For both, it is
the first time venturing beyond the familiar landmarks that
define their lives, and there is no mistaking the journey's symbolic significance: it is a test of whether the centripetal force of
the neighborhood can be escaped. Lila, predictably, is the ring-
leader, as Elena recalls:

"We held each other by the hand, we walked side by side,
but for me, as usual, it was as if Lila were ten steps ahead and
knew precisely what to do, where to go. I was used to feeling second in everything, and so I was sure that to her, who had always
been first, everything was clear: the pace, the calculation of the
time available for going and coming back, the route that would
take us to the sea ... I abandoned myself happily."

Yet when it starts to rain, surprisingly, it is Lila who wants
to turn back, and Elena who tries to convince her to keep going.
It is a foreshadowing of the two girls' destinies, as Elena finds
within herself the strength to escape, while Lila's even greater
strength seems paralyzed by the prospect of leaving home.

By the time we reach the third book, the friends seem to have
become opposites in every way. Elena is a cultured bourgeois living in Florence, in Italy's wealthy North, while Lila, after an early
marriage and tumultuous affair, has been reduced to working

98   in a sausage factory in Naples, in the country's poor, backward South. This polarity of north and south, so deeply ingrained in Italian politics and culture, is Ferrante's avenue for approaching one of the central themes of the global novel—the geographical disparity of wealth and power. Because Italy contains within its own borders the same rivalry of North and South that is also writ large on the globe itself, it is a perfect laboratory for exploring how these differences determine the course of individual lives.

Yet Ferrante is not certain that geographical differences, and the class differences they encode, are really as determinative as they seem. For, like entangled particles in quantum physics, Elena and Lila end up reflecting and influencing one another even at a distance. This is especially the case when it comes to love and marriage, where both friends end up living out the impossible contradictions of male-female relations in an era of great social change. As children, the girls observe the decline of Melina Cappuccio, a mentally unbalanced woman in the neighborhood who is jilted by her married lover, the blithe womanizer Donato Sarratore. In a scene that will become a touchstone throughout the series, Lila is transfixed by seeing Melina walking down the street eating soap, a sign that she has become fully deranged by love and powerlessness.

Years later, both Lila and Elena will fall in love with Donato's son Nino; as the story progresses, each woman ends up leaving her husband for him. Yet both end up abandoned by Nino, who for all his professed political radicalism remains a chauvinist when it comes to how he treats women, and in his cavalier attitude toward raising his own children. Both are forced into the position of Melina, driven almost to ruin by the love of a worthless

man. For Elena, this humiliation is especially acute, since it represents the victory of the tradition of female dependency over
her adult commitment to feminist liberation, which is one of the
major themes of her own writing. "Was I lying to myself when I
portrayed myself as free and autonomous?" she asks. "And was
I lying to my audience when I played the part of someone who,
with her two small books, had sought to help every woman con-
fess what she couldn't say to herself? Were they mere formulas
that it was convenient for me to believe in while in fact I was no
different from my more traditional contemporaries?"

There's no doubt that the shape Elena's life takes is quite
different from those of her uneducated peers. After all, she is
the one who ends up writing the story we are reading, a feat
that none of the other characters could undertake. In this sense,
Elena's emancipation from the neighborhood is confirmed by
her ability to understand the neighborhood "from above," in a
position of superiority that is made possible by her development of a global consciousness. The mere fact of traveling
abroad already separates Elena from her early friends, including
Lila, who spends her life without ever boarding an airplane. As
an author, on the other hand, Elena has the chance to visit France
and Germany, even the United States, and she writes about the
almost physical sense of expansion that her world undergoes
while traveling: "It was an extraordinary experience. I felt again
that I had no limits, I was capable of flying over oceans, expand-
ing over the entire world: an exhilarating delirium."

This physical mobility is a reflection of the intellectual
freedom that Elena earns through her decades of study. As a
teenager, we see her entering tentatively and self-consciously

100   into the realm of politics and ideas. She is initially uncertain
of the language to use in such discussions, and can only parrot
back phrases and formulas she hears from her more confident
friends, including Nino Sarratore. She suffers a setback early on,
when she writes an article about a conflict at her school over
religious instruction, which Nino promises to get published in
a left-wing newspaper. His failure to do so leaves Elena shaken
about her abilities as a writer. Not until many years and hundreds of pages have passed does she learn that, in fact, Nino
destroyed the article out of jealousy, recognizing that Elena
wrote better than he did. It is a small example of the obstacles
she has to face on the road to becoming an independent thinker,
equal to the better-educated, more privileged men who intimi-
date and undermine her. Indeed, Elena's feminist awakening
comes in part from her realization that her very academic success was owed to her ability to adopt male ways of thinking and
speaking—a kind of camouflage, which she rejects after reading
feminist theory in the 1970s.

In all these ways, Elena's story seems like a story about
liberation—from poverty, from parochialism, from female sub-
ordination, in short from everything represented in the novel by
"dialect." Yet because she remains connected with Lila, and regularly alternates the story of her friend's life with her own, we
see that liberation is also possible in very different terms from
those Elena pursues. At her lowest moments, Lila is much worse
off than Elena could ever be. She is married as a teenager to a
husband who beats and rapes her; she works for a corrupt boss in
a dangerous factory; and she is constantly at war with the Solara
brothers, the criminals who dominate the neighborhood. By the

end of the book, however, Lila turns out to have fashioned her own destiny, perhaps more successfully than Elena. She marries a respectful new husband, learns how to write software code, and opens a profitable computer consulting business, even as she remains in the old neighborhood, speaking the old dialect.

It is only at the very end of the saga, when Lila's young daughter Tina vanishes—whether kidnapped or killed, and why, she and the reader never learn—that her self-fashioning is conclusively torpedoed by the violent legacy of the past. Violence against girls and women turns out to be the ultimate deciding factor in these lives, a danger that can be warded off neither by Lila's force of personality nor by Elena's disciplined self-improvement. For all of Elena's achievements, then, her final verdict on the possibility of liberation—from the past, the neighborhood, the life of fear—is a negative one: "I had fled, in fact. Only to discover, in the decades to come, that I had been wrong, that it was a chain with larger and larger links: the neighborhood was connected to the city, the city to Italy, Italy to Europe, Europe to the whole planet. And this is how I see it today: it's not the neighborhood that's sick, it's not Naples, it's the entire earth, it's the universe, or universes. And shrewdness means hiding and hiding from oneself the true state of things."

Ferrante suggests that the local, while it may appear to be the opposite of the global, is actually its necessary complement. In the Neapolitan novels, Naples itself remains the matrix on which all of Elena Greco's experience is formed. The lessons about power and violence she absorbed as a child in the neighborhood are not refuted, merely amplified, by the political terrorism she experiences in the 1970s, in the age of the Red Brigades, and by

102   the corruption exposed in the 1990s, when Nino—now a mem-
ber of Parliament—is caught up in Tangentopoli, the bribery
scandal that rocked Italian politics. Ferrante's interweaving
of fictional events with historical landmarks—in addition to
Tangentopoli, the characters discuss or experience the assassination of former prime minister Aldo Moro in 1978, the Naples
earthquake of 1980, and the terrorist attacks of September 11,
2001—is a further way of tying the neighborhood to a larger
national and international context.

By the end of the series, however, we find Lila embarked
on an obsessive antiquarian study of Naples's own history and
landmarks, as if to suggest that the city of her birth already
contained all the history she needed to experience: "a permanent stream of splendors and miseries, a cyclical Naples where
everything was marvelous and everything became gray and
irrational and everything sparkled again." This sense of history as fate echoes Elena's own conclusion about Naples: "To
be born in that city . . . is useful for only one thing: to have
always known, almost instinctively, what today, with end-
less fine distinctions, everyone is beginning to claim: that the
dream of unlimited progress is in reality a nightmare of sav-
agery and death."

In this way, the local, even parochial perspective of the
Neapolitan novels turns out to echo the apocalyptic judgments and uncanny intuitions of many different writers—from
Houellebecq and Atwood to Bolaño and Murakami—who
address the global more directly. And this suggests, once again,
that in fiction the local and the global exist in a relationship,
not of opposition, but of dialectical tension. Even in an age

of globalization, most lives—especially, most childhoods—
remain confined to the context of neighborhood, city, and
region. Stories like the ones told by Adichie and Hamid, of lives
lived across borders, remain exceptional, which is one reason
why they are fascinating.

But whether their story encompasses the cosmos, a conti-
nent, or a city block, these novelists see individual fates in an
international perspective. Strikingly, for many of the writers
we have examined, it is the experience of violence, especially
violence against women, that provides the bridge between individual stories and global judgments. Atwood's Oryx, a victim
of sex trafficking, calls out to the hundreds of women murdered
in Bolaño's Santa Teresa, who in turn recognize the experience
of prostitution suffered by Adichie's Ifemelu, and the domestic
abuse undergone by Ferrante's Lila, and the suicidal resistance
of Pamuk's headscarf girls.

Violence against women is not a new theme in either life
or literature, of course; it has been part of the DNA of the novel
since *Clarissa*. But there is something striking about the una-
nimity of these very different writers, representatives of so
many languages and nations, when it comes to the significance
of misogyny and sexualized violence today. In this crime, such
writers invite us to identify the cardinal sins of our time—
cruelty, exploitation, inequality. This convergence suggests
that the global novel may be, not the homogenizing and coer-
cive force it has often been called, but the herald and agent of a
dawning collective conscience. Everyone must strive to hasten
its approach.

FURTHER READING

Adichie, Chimamanda Ngozi, *Americanah* (New York: Anchor, 2014)

Apter, Emily, *Against World Literature* (New York: Verso, 2013)

Atwood, Margaret, *Oryx and Crake* (New York: Anchor, 2004)

Bolaño, Roberto, *2666* (New York: Picador, 2009)

Casanova, Pascale, *The World Republic of Letters*, trans. M. B. DeBevoise (Cambridge, MA: Harvard University Press, 2007)

Ferrante, Elena, *My Brilliant Friend*, trans. Ann Goldstein, (New York: Europa Editions, 2012)

——, *The Story of a New Name*, trans. Ann Goldstein (New York: Europa Editions, 2013)

——, *Those Who Leave and Those Who Stay,* trans. Ann Goldstein (New York: Europa Editions, 2014)

——, *The Story of the Lost Child,* trans. Ann Goldstein (New York: Europa Editions, 2015)

Hamid, Mohsin, *The Reluctant Fundamentalist* (New York: Harvest, 2008)

Houellebecq, Michel, *The Possibility of an Island*, trans. Gavin Bowd (New York: Vintage, 2007)

Mizumura, Minae, *The Fall of Language in the Age of English*, trans. Mari Yoshihara (New York: Columbia University Press, 2015)

Murakami, Haruki, *1Q84,* trans. Jay Rubin (New York: Vintage, 2013)

Pamuk, Orhan, *Snow*, trans. Maureen Freely (New York: Vintage, 2005)

Columbia Global Reports is a publishing imprint from Columbia University that commissions authors to do original on-site reporting around the globe on a wide range of issues. The resulting novella-length books offer new ways to look at and understand the world that can be read in a few hours. Most readers are curious and busy. Our books are for them.
globalreports.columbia.edu